COMPUTER
SCIENCE

BCS, THE CHARTERED INSTITUTE FOR IT

BCS, The Chartered Institute for IT champions the global IT profession and the interests of individuals engaged in that profession for the benefit of all. We promote wider social and economic progress through the advancement of information technology, science and practice. We bring together industry, academics, practitioners and government to share knowledge, promote new thinking, inform the design of new curricula, shape public policy and inform the public.

Our vision is to be a world-class organisation for IT. Our 70,000 strong membership includes practitioners, businesses, academics and students in the UK and internationally. We deliver a range of professional development tools for practitioners and employees. A leading IT qualification body, we offer a range of widely recognised qualifications.

Further Information
BCS, The Chartered Institute for IT,
First Floor, Block D,
North Star House, North Star Avenue,
Swindon, SN2 1FA, United Kingdom.
T +44 (0) 1793 417 424
F +44 (0) 1793 417 444
www.bcs.org/contact

http://shop.bcs.org/

COMPUTER SCIENCE TEACHER
Insight into the computing classroom

Beverly Clarke

Published by BCS Learning & Development Ltd, a wholly owned subsidiary of BCS, The Chartered Institute for IT, First Floor, Block D, North Star House, North Star Avenue, Swindon, SN2 1FA, UK. www.bcs.org

ISBN: 978-1-78017-394-8
PDF ISBN: 978-1-78017-395-5
ePUB ISBN: 978-1-78017-396-2
Kindle ISBN: 978-1-78017-397-9

Ebook available

British Cataloguing in Publication Data.
A CIP catalogue record for this book is available at the British Library.

Disclaimer:
The views expressed in this book are of the author and do not necessarily reflect the views of the Institute or BCS Learning & Development Ltd except where explicitly stated as such. Although every care has been taken by the author(s) and BCS Learning & Development Ltd in the preparation of the publication, no warranty is given by the author or BCS Learning & Development Ltd as publisher as to the accuracy or completeness of the information contained within it and neither the author nor BCS Learning & Development Ltd shall be responsible or liable for any loss or damage whatsoever arising by virtue of such information or any instructions or advice contained within this publication or by any of the aforementioned.

BCS books are available at special quantity discounts to use as premiums and sale promotions, or for use in corporate training programmes. Please visit our Contact Us page at www.bcs.org/contact

Typeset by Lapiz Digital Services, Chennai, India.
Printed and bound by Henry Ling Limited, at the Dorset Press, Dorchester, DT1 1HD

CONTENTS

CONTENTS

LIST OF FIGURES AND TABLES

AUTHOR

Beverly Clarke started her computing career working in IT support for a county council. This was followed by further roles in IT support for corporate IT companies. Upon becoming a mother, Beverly found that she wanted to give something back to the computing and IT community and changed career direction; she undertook an evening course in teaching and found it enjoyable and rewarding. In 2001, she began working as a sessional lecturer at a college in adult education.

With a keen interest in teaching, Beverly undertook her Postgraduate Certificate in Education (PGCE) and then obtained qualified teacher status (QTS). This then led to a job as Deputy Head of IT in a secondary school. After three years, the position of Head of IT/Computing arose. This also coincided with major changes to the National Curriculum. A part of the job description was to ensure that the department was equipped to deal with the changes. Beverly felt she could make a difference and successfully applied for the job. Having graduated with a degree in Computing Studies and not used it fully in education and seeing pupils leaving schools and colleges with only an understanding of certain packages and applications but lacking skills and knowledge for the information age, Beverly decided to get involved with Computing At School (CAS) to see how she could play a part to ensure that the new curriculum was a success. She also undertook additional study and became a CAS Master Teacher.

Always a self-starter, Beverly then launched and maintained a CAS Hub. She set about contacting all local schools to spread the news about the curriculum – including resources and building a networking community. She ran a very successful CAS Hub and this was featured in a Department for Education (DfE) video.

During her secondary school career, Beverly then gained the position of Director of Computing and Digital Literacy. She led a successful department, achieving outstanding and best of school results at key stage 4, year on year. Beverly has also collaborated with national educational websites and European colleagues, advising teachers on aspects of the new curriculum. She was also the educational consultant for a series of BBC Bitesize computational thinking videos for key stage 3.

Beverly also delivered training sessions in collaboration with BCS, The Chartered Institute for IT to BCS scholars on managing a department through change, getting that first job and getting through the interview process. Additionally, she has interviewed prospective candidates for the BCS Scholarship scheme.

She has worked on sharing of good practice teams as a leader of Teaching and Learning. Beverly is National Professional Qualification for Senior Leadership (NPQSL) qualified, having led on successful whole-school projects. Having achieved the level of NPQSL, she decided to work in another part of education and get involved in ensuring that teachers had the correct materials to deliver the computing curriculum. This led to further collaboration with BCS, as a subject matter expert.

Her inspiration for computing in general grows from living in different countries (Guyana – South America, The Bahamas and England) during her formative years and being able to appreciate countries without technological advances as well as those which had greater technological advances, and seeing the benefits and transformation that technology gives from one generation to the next.

FOREWORD

Recent changes to the national curriculums of England and other countries have seen an increased focus on computer science. These changes have raised a host of questions around what is meant by computing education and what it means to be a teacher in this subject area. Beverly's book is a timely guide to help us navigate this exciting field. It supports those in the profession whether they be head teachers looking to support the subject in their schools, experienced computing teachers, or teachers who trained in a different discipline. And, maybe more importantly, it demystifies the subject for those thinking about starting a career as a computer science teacher.

Computing is changing the way we interact with and see the world. Whatever forms the careers of the future take, it is likely that the students of today will be using computers in their workplace. Preparing students to create, interact with and adapt to technology lies at the heart of any 21st-century education and the computing curriculum is well placed to support this. We can't sensibly assume that students come pre-programmed to use computers safely and effectively; for most students, it will be teachers who open their eyes to the possibilities that computing offers.

However, two worrying trends have coincided with the introduction of the computing curriculum to England. Firstly, a decrease in the numbers of teachers applying for computing training roles. Without new educators entering the profession the opportunities that computing offers will be hidden from those who could make most use of them. And secondly, a decrease in the access to digital qualifications for female students and those from poorer backgrounds.

If you are considering becoming a computer science teacher, you are looking at one of the most exciting and rewarding jobs imaginable, in one of the most dynamic and important subject areas. This book will offer you plenty of advice on what it takes to enter and succeed in the profession. If you're a current computer science teacher, computing teacher or school practitioner interested in computing, the practical advice in this book will help you understand better how to implement a successful and inclusive computing curriculum.

Peter Kemp
University of Roehampton
May 2017

ACKNOWLEDGEMENTS

The author would like to acknowledge and thank the following for their contributions toward the content of this book. My parents, daughters, family and friends. Andrew Csizmadia – Newman University, Louise Duncan – Sunbury Manor School, Steve Clarke – Therfield School, Richard Williams – Bradley Stoke Community School, Peter Kemp – Roehampton University, Kathie Drake – Stepgates Community School, Pauline Clarke – St Antony's Catholic Primary School, Jayne Fenton-Hall – Sunbury Manor School, Chris Sharples – Lady Lumley's School, Steven Gibson – Glen Park Primary School, Veronica Clarke – West Ham Church School, Dr Irene Bell – Stranmillis University College, Charlotte Amalie for photo taking and Pete Dando for photo editing. Along with wider BCS and CAS colleagues, who provided inspiration, accuracy checking and being sounding boards.

ABBREVIATIONS

A-level   Advanced level

BCS   British Computer Society

BTEC   Business and Technology Education Council

CAS   Computing At School

CATS   Cognitive Ability Tests

CCEA   Council for Curriculum, Examinations and Assessment

COIN   Communication and Interaction Needs

CPD   Continuing Professional Development

CPU   Central Processing Unit

CSTA   Computer Science Teachers Association

CT   Computational Thinking

EAL   English as an Additional Language

Ebacc   English Baccalaureate

EHCP   Education Health and Care Plans

EMS   Enhanced Mainstream School

EYFS   Early Years Foundation Stage

GCE   General Certificate of Education

GCSE   General Certificate of Secondary Education

GTP   Graduate Teacher Programme

GUI	Graphical User Interface
ICT	Information and communication technology
IWB	Interactive White Boards
LRC	Learning Resource Centre
LSA	Learning Support Assistant
MAC	Media Access Control
MOOC	Massive Open Online Course
MPS	Main Pay Scale
NAACE	National Association of Advisors for Computers in Education
NPQH	National Professional Qualification for Headship
NPQML	National Professional Qualification for Middle Leadership
NPQSL	National Professional Qualification for Senior Leadership
NQT	Newly qualified teachers
OFSTED	Office for Standards in Education
O-level	Ordinary level
PD	Physically disabled
PGCE	Postgraduate Certificate in Education
PPA	Planning, Preparation and Assessment
QTS	Qualified teacher status
SATs	Standard Attainment Tests
SDP	School Development Plan
SEN	Special Educational Needs
SFIA	Skills Framework for the Information Age
SLT	Senior Leadership Team

STEAM   Science, Technology, Engineering, Arts, Mathematics

STEM   Science, Technology, Engineering, Mathematics

TA   Teaching Assistant

T-levels Technical levels

VLE   Virtual Learning Environment

GLOSSARY

Artificial intelligence The study of computers being able to perform tasks usually only associated with humans, such as voice recognition and decision making.

Assessing pupil progress Describes methods used to consistently check if pupils are making progress.

Autonomous systems A collection of systems that are all controlled at the same time from a single point.

Big Data A term used to describe very large data sets.

Bitcoin A term used to describe a digital cryptocurrency and payment system.

Boolean operators These are used to connect search terms to give better results.

CAS Hub A term used to describe education professionals, meeting to discuss and share ideas on developing the teaching of the computing curriculum.

CAS Hub Leader A teacher who hosts CAS events for local teachers to attend.

CAS Master Teacher A teacher who has undertaken specialist training to teach the new computing curriculum.

CAS Network of Excellence (NoE) A national community of professional practice, covering schools, universities, IT employers and professional bodies.

Cloud computing A term for using the internet to provide services.

Computational thinking   Term used to describe a set of cognitive and problem solving skills.

Computer Aided Design   Term used to describe software that is used to design and draw technical plans, such as for a construction project.

Controlled assessment   A form of assessment that is marked by teachers in school and then sampled by the awarding body.

Curriculum   The subjects that are studied in an educational organisation.

Cybersecurity   Protection of computer systems from online attacks.

Debug   The process of finding and correcting errors in programs.

Devices   Term used to describe input, output and backing storage that can be connected to a computer system.

Digital age   The current period in which we live that is characterised by computerised systems.

Digital literacy   The knowledge to choose and use hardware, software and the internet, safely, efficiently, responsibly and confidently.

Diversity   The study of pupils with differences and celebrating these distinctions in the classroom.

Dyslexia Quality Mark   External and international quality mark that shows an organisation is providing for and supporting individuals with dyslexia.

Form tutor   A teacher who is responsible for the pastoral care of his or her pupils on a daily basis.

Formative assessment   Methods undertaken by teachers during learning to ascertain pupil understanding.

Gifted and Talented   Describes pupils who display knowledge and skills significantly beyond their age and stage.

Hardware   The physical parts of a computer system.

Inclusion The study of including all pupils within the classroom.

Internet An international communication system linking computers through a variety of telecommunications links.

Internet of Things (IoT) The connection of all types of devices to the internet, which send and receive data.

Kinaesthetic activity A learning style which focuses on physical activity.

Lesson observation A formal or informal check on teaching and learning in the classroom.

Lesson plan A detailed plan that shows how a teacher will approach a lesson and what the learners will achieve.

More Able Describes pupils who display knowledge and skills significantly beyond their age and stage.

Pastoral A term used to describe those activities that are not academic, such as emotion, spiritual and personal needs support.

Physical computing A term used to describe hands-on methods of conducting computing lessons.

Plenary A short activity at the end of a lesson to pull together learning.

Plugged An activity which uses computers.

Programme of study Explains the aims of the curriculum, attainment targets and subject content for each key stage.

Progress grid A way of checking on pupil progress.

Pupil premium Additional funding for publicly-funded schools in England to raise the attainment of disadvantaged pupils of all abilities and to close the gaps between them and their peers.

Python A text-based programming language.

Quantum computers A term used to describe theoretical computers, which work on 'qubits' as opposed to 'bits'. They make use of subatomic particles and each bit can hold more than 0 or 1.

Risk assessment   A form which details any risks that can occur when doing an activity such as a school trip; these range from fire, lost pupils, terror threat, transport issues, illness, and so on.

Safeguarding   Actions taken to protect all from neglect, abuse and harm to ensure all are safe.

School Development Plan   A detailed plan that shows strategic improvement that the school will take over a finite time period.

School Improvement Priority   Issues that a school deems to be of great importance that will appear on the School Development Plan.

Scratch   A visual programming language.

Seating plan   A drawn plan which identifies where pupils sit in a classroom.

Software   Programs and applications that can be run on a computer system.

Staffroom   A dedicated room in an educational institution where staff can meet.

Starter activity   A short activity at the start of a lesson.

Summative assessment   Undertaken at the end of a unit of work that is compared against a benchmark to check on pupil attainment.

Teachers' union   An organisation which protects the rights of teachers.

Union representative   A member of staff who works on behalf of the teachers' union.

Unplugged   An activity that is conducted without computers.

PREFACE

The purpose of this book is to explore the role of a computer science or computing teacher and to give guidance. While written mainly through state secondary school eyes, there are references to primary education. There are supporting quotes and case studies from practising teachers across key stages 1–5, with varying degrees of experience.

The audience for this book is wide. It is relevant for those considering entering the teaching profession, trainee and newly qualified teachers (NQTs), heads of departments, head teachers, recruiters, university educators, careers services, career changers, IT professionals and anyone else interested in the specifics around being a computer science teacher. The reader will gain an understanding of how this subject came to be, its relevance, the attributes, knowledge and skills required by a computer science teacher. For example, the reader will appreciate that being a computer science teacher is part of a much bigger picture within the school environment. Each school is different, however, there are transferable skills, knowledge and attributes that will make the computer science teacher successful within any teaching and educational environment.

Tools, methods and techniques required to be a successful teacher and to support the teacher are also discussed. The standards for the teaching profession are also examined. For the trainee new to the profession, there is a focus on analysing computer science teacher job adverts with a view to supporting the teacher in gaining a teaching position. Attention is also drawn to managing the computing classroom environment.

There is a focus on challenging stereotypes within computer science by looking at promoting the subject to groups such as girls who traditionally tend to be under-represented in this subject area. There are references provided for the teacher to ensure the classroom is diverse and inclusive.

The reader will appreciate that being a subject specialist is not the only thing that makes a teacher successful. The book will show the reader that teaching is a rewarding career and will discuss ways to progress in a teaching career. Through the case studies, the reader will learn about the experiences of career changers, implementation of the curriculum, school life and progression through the employment field.

Relevant standards in computer science and teaching are referenced and the reader is encouraged to undertake the self-assessment activities in the book, along with further reading.

Additionally, the reader will see the relevance of the subject in preparing young people for the future as we live in a fast changing technological world. This book seeks to support all those involved in delivering knowledge in a world where technology and the advancements of people are currently at the fastest they have ever been.

1 INTRODUCTION TO TEACHING SECONDARY COMPUTER SCIENCE

This chapter explores the background of the current computing national curriculum in England and discusses terminology used around the curriculum. Comparisons are made between the English national curriculum and that of the other parts of the United Kingdom (UK) and the United States of America (USA). There is also comparison of the UK education systems.

AN EVOLVING SUBJECT

Computers! Digital! Technology! Apps! Online! Cyber! We hear these words all around us. This is a part of everyday terminology that did not exist a century ago. There are new words being added to dictionaries every year. We use a multitude of devices and software and we demand more from technology than ever before. With these demands comes a question. Who is teaching our young people to use and design appropriate technology for this digital age?

This is where the computer science teacher comes in. The computer science teacher is skilled in computing knowledge and understands the new national curriculum in England and the computing programme of study (published September 2013).

At this early stage, you may have noticed the words 'computer science' and 'computing'. Before we go any further let's clarify the difference between these terms.

WHAT IS COMPUTER SCIENCE?

Computer science can be described as 'the scientific and practical study of computation'[1] and problem solving. In the computing programme of study, computer science is described as the '**the core of computing**'.

At the centre of computer science is computational thinking (CT) (algorithmic design, abstraction, decomposition, pattern recognition, pattern generalisation), which assists in problem solving, system design and artificial intelligence, all of which are of importance to the economy and for citizens to function. A computer science teacher will guide a pupil through the strands of CT and teach pupils to be digitally literate through theoretical and practical activity, thus equipping the pupil to be functional in this newly emerging world.

WHAT IS COMPUTING?

Computing is the collective name given in the curriculum to three areas, one of which is computer science. The three areas are:

- computer science (foundations);
- information and communication technology (ICT) (applications);
- digital literacy (implications).[2]

We've covered computer science already; let's look at the other two.

ICT is where one is a user of systems at an application level, by manipulating images in software, manipulating data and sending emails, for example (up to 2012, England's curriculum was an ICT curriculum).

Digital literacy looks at safe usage and navigation of the digital world.

Within a school, the computer science teacher is involved in teaching computing, and it is 'computing', as an umbrella term, to which the national curriculum now refers. On a school timetable, the subject will often be referred to as computing, although you will find that some schools use the terms 'computer science' and 'computing' interchangeably.

This book mainly focuses on the teacher of computer science, as computer science is the prominent addition to the English computing curriculum, but should also be a valuable resource for the computing teacher.

Computer science is the area of focus as it has not previously been taught and teachers need to upskill to teach this area. Additionally, the skills and knowledge gained through studying computer science, as the core of computing, enable pupils to learn how computer systems work, how they are designed and programmed; this is important as computer systems are becoming more and more integral to our lives.

THE COMPUTING CURRICULUM

Figure 1.1 compares ICT (the old curriculum) and computer science (the core of the current computing curriculum). Remember this is a fairly new subject on the curriculum, and it is important to be clear about the differences since at times, as a computer science teacher, you will be educating beyond the classroom, to other colleagues and into the community, such as at parents' evening. Figure 1.1 is taken from the Computing At School (CAS), National Association of Advisors for Computers in Education (Naace), Association for Information Technology in Teacher Education (ITTE) Joint Statement, June 2012.[3]

Figure 1.1 Comparison of ICT and computer science

Information and communication technology	Computer science
The study of computers and how they are used	The study of how computer systems are built and work
Human need is central to the subject	Computation is central to the subject
Concerned with the design, development and evaluation of systems, with particular emphasis on the data, functional and usability requirements of end users	Concerned with algorithmic thinking and the ways in which a real world problem can be decomposed in order to construct a working solution
Focuses on building or programming a solution by a combination of currently available devices and software	Solves problems and develops new systems by writing new software and developing innovative and computational approaches
Emphasis on selecting, evaluating, designing and configuring appropriate software and devices. Programming is one method of creating desired outcomes	Emphasis on principles and techniques for building new software and designing new hardware. Programming and coding is a central technique to create outcomes
ICT supports, enhances and empowers human activity and informs future developments	Computation is a lens through which we can understand the natural world and the nature of thought itself in a new way
Trending towards the higher level study and application of ICT in a range of contexts, from academic to vocational	Trending towards the higher level academic study of computing and computer science

We will now examine the aims of the current National Curriculum in England, as described in the computing programme of study – Figure 1.2.

Figure 1.2 Aims of the National Curriculum in computing

The National Curriculum for Computing aims to ensure that all pupils:

- can understand and apply the fundamental principles and concepts of computer science, including abstraction, logic, algorithms and data representation;

- can analyse problems in computational terms, and have repeated practical experience of writing computer programs in order to solve such problems;

- can evaluate and apply information technology, including new or unfamiliar technologies, analytically to solve problems;

- are responsible, competent, confident and creative users of information and communication technology.

Source: https://www.gov.uk/government/publications/national-curriculum-in-england-computing-programmes-of-study/national-curriculum-in-england-computing-programmes-of-study

Here you will notice the mention of computer science concepts, writing of programs, application of information technology and being a responsible user of technology. This is computing, the collective areas you will teach.

There is another reason why computer science is of such importance in the curriculum. Computer science is listed as a science in the Ebacc (English Baccalaureate). This is a performance measure against which secondary schools are measured and is used as a means to raise standards across all schools in England.[4]

If you are a primary teacher reader of this book, or are seeking to become one, you may well ask, how is this content relevant to me? The answer is simple: grades obtained at primary level, during the year 6 Standard Attainment Tests (SATs) or given by a primary teacher, are used alongside other data to generate progress and attainment predictions for pupils[5] at the end of key stage 4. Thus, being aware of the importance that you play within the education system is essential. Additionally, many primary schools are increasingly having specialist single subject computer science staff. Even if you are not a single subject teacher in a primary school, the cross-curricular links and wider computing picture are very relevant. Chapter 3 looks at Progress 8 and Attainment 8 measures which chart a pupil's journey from primary through to the end of secondary school which is useful for all teachers.

The origins of the computing curriculum

How did the new computing curriculum come about? What were the drivers?

In order to address these questions, one must look back to January 2012, where at the BETT Education Show, the Rt Hon. Michael Gove MP, then Education Secretary, gave a speech on ICT in the curriculum – Figure 1.3.

Figure 1.3 Rt Hon. Michael Gove speech at the BETT Show, 2012

'Almost every field of employment now depends on technology. From radio, to television, computers and the internet, each new technological advance has changed our world and changed us too. But there is one notable exception – Education has barely changed.'

'The fundamental model of school education is still a teacher talking to a group of pupils. It has barely changed over the centuries, even since Plato established the earliest "academia" in a shady olive grove in ancient Athens.'

(Continued)

Figure 1.3 (Continued)

> 'Technology is already bringing about a profound transformation in education, in ways that we can see before our very eyes and in others that we haven't even dreamt of yet.'
>
> 'Our school system has not prepared children for this new world. Millions have left school over the past decade without even the basics they need for a decent job. And the current curriculum cannot prepare British students to work at the very forefront of technological change.'
>
> 'We need to improve the training of teachers so that they have the skills and knowledge they need to make the most of the opportunities ahead.'
>
> 'Following submissions to the national curriculum review by organisations such as the British Computer Society, Computing at School, eSkills UK, Naace and the Royal Society, all called the current National Curriculum for ICT unsatisfactory, as the ICT curriculum did not stretch pupils enough or allow enough opportunities for innovation and experimentation.'

Source: https://www.gov.uk/government/speeches/michael-gove-speech-at-the-bett-show-2012

Following this speech, the ICT programme of study was withdrawn from September 2012, with plans for a new computing curriculum to be delivered from September 2014. The aim being to encourage the professionalism of teachers in deciding approaches and resources to best teach the computing curriculum.

To enable this innovation there was a massive need to equip teachers with the subject knowledge and tools to teach the new curriculum, ensuring pupils possessed the necessary skills to compete with other countries and to lead the way in technological advances. This gave way to the computing and computer science courses that we have today.

You will note in the extract from the speech that there is reference to a number of organisations. What will now follow is a brief background of two of these organisations which assisted in leading the way with the new computing curriculum, as examples of relevant bodies that may be of interest.

Computing At School (CAS)

CAS was one of the organisations that submitted proposals for a change to this curriculum. CAS is the subject association for all computing teachers and is partnered with BCS, The Chartered Institute for IT (previously 'The British Computer Society').

Figure 1.4 CAS purpose and mission statement

'CAS was born out of our excitement with our discipline, combined with a serious concern that many students are being turned off computing by a combination of factors that have conspired to make the subject seem dull and pedestrian. Our goal is to put the excitement back into Computing at school.'

'The mission of Computing At School is to provide leadership and strategic guidance to all those involved in Computing education in schools, with a significant but not exclusive focus on the Computer Science theme within the wider Computing curriculum. Excellence in the teaching of Computing can only be made by teachers through the way they deliver the skills, knowledge, understanding and attitudes associated with the curriculum.'

'CAS are a collaborative partner with the BCS through the BCS Academy of Computing, and have formal support from other industry partners. Membership is open to almost everyone, and is very broad, including teachers, parents, governors, exam boards, industry, professional societies, and universities.'

Source: www.computingatschool.org.uk/about

CAS started off as a grassroots group and quickly became the 'voice' behind the new curriculum. Figure 1.4 shows a few quotes from the CAS website to give an understanding of what CAS is about.

If you are not currently a CAS member it is recommended that you sign up to keep abreast of changes and updates within computing.

The Royal Society

'The Royal Society[6] is a Fellowship of many of the world's most eminent scientists and is the oldest scientific academy in continuous existence'.[7] The Royal Society published their influential report **'Shut down or restart?'** in January 2012. There are few key points in this report to which I wish to draw your attention (Figure 1.5).

Figure 1.5 Royal Society report

- 'There is a shortage of teachers who are able to teach beyond basic digital literacy.'
- 'There is a lack of continuing professional development for teachers of Computing.'
- 'Every child should have the opportunity to learn Computing at school, including exposure to Computer Science as a rigorous academic discipline.'
- 'There is a need for qualifications in aspects of Computing that are accessible at school level but are not currently taught. There is also a need for existing inappropriate assessment methods to be updated.'
- 'There is a need for augmentation and coordination of current Enhancement and Enrichment activities to support the study of Computing.'

Source: https://royalsociety.org/~/media/education/computing-in-schools/2012-01-12-computing-in-schools.pdf

Through these quotes you will see where and how the need for the computer science specialism arose. In the references section of the report (curriculum changes), there are recommended links for further reading.

ENGLISH NATIONAL CURRICULUM VERSUS OTHER COUNTRIES

One of the key points of the national curriculum is that the government says it will allow 'teachers greater flexibility to respond to pupil needs'[8] and it is a curriculum of freedom and autonomy, where teachers will 'be allowed to cover truly innovative, specialist and challenging topics'.[9] With the national curriculum, it is hoped that pupils in England will be able to catch up and compete with the world's best pupils and education systems. Depending on which literature you read, England/the UK is either listed in the top 10 or top 20 of the world's best education systems. However, it is still a national goal to get to the top of such rankings. Bear in mind that rankings of this nature consider a variety of different factors. The Pearson report,[10] for example, draws on data from the Organisation for Economic Co-operation and Development (OECD)[11] to arrive at the world's top education systems.

Within the UK (comprising England, Wales, Northern Ireland and Scotland), there are differing national curriculums. This book looks at the English national curriculum; however, it is worth looking at the other curriculums in the UK and also that of one of the world's leading countries, the USA, for comparison.

Wales

At the time of writing,[12] the Welsh curriculum is under review, with a new Welsh curriculum coming into place from September 2018, to affect all 3- to 16-year-olds. The reasons behind this change are as with the English national curriculum: to help young people to adapt to the changing world around them. Back in 2013, there was a report into ICT in Wales and this was documented in the 'The ICT Steering Group's report to the Welsh Government'. Some of the key findings of this report are shown in Figure 1.6.

Figure 1.6 The ICT Steering Group's report to the Welsh Government

- A new subject named Computing should be created to replace Information and Communications Technology (ICT) from Foundation Phase onwards. This new subject will disaggregate into two main areas: Computer Science (CS); and Information Technology (IT).

- Computing should be integrated into the curriculum as the fourth science, served by a mandatory Programme of Study, and receive the same status as the other three sciences.

- A Statutory Digital Literacy (DL) Framework should be implemented to work alongside the Literacy and Numeracy Framework from Foundation Phase through to post-16 education.

- Perceptions of Computing education pathways should be changed to recognise the key societal roles of computing and technology, as well as promote the importance and diversity of IT careers.

- The revised Computing curriculum should encourage creativity, allow thematic working and develop real world problem-solving. It should be flexible enough to continually evolve to remain current, adopting an Agile ideology and approach to ensure this.

- Engagement and collaboration between education and industry should be an integral part of the curriculum to embed current practices and skills.

- Pathways for Initial Teacher Training (ITT) in Computing should be created to encourage the best talent into the profession. All entrants to the teaching profession should have the skills to deliver the Digital Literacy Framework (DLF).

- A programme of training and professional development to enable the new Computing curriculum should be accessible to new and existing teachers.

Source: http://learning.gov.wales/docs/learningwales/publications/131003-ict-steering-group-report-en.pdf[13]

To keep up-to-date with changes to the Welsh curriculum, it is advisable to follow the CAS group, CAS Wales, for up-to-date information and support with the curriculum.

Northern Ireland

Currently in Northern Ireland, Using ICT (UICT) is still on the national curriculum and not computing. UICT is a cross-curricular skill and schools must ensure that all pupils have opportunities to acquire and develop this skill. Within the 'Desirable Features' of UICT there are opportunities to undertake programming. The degree to which this is achieved will probably depend on the individual teachers' knowledge.

However, change is happening! Awarding bodies are reviewing current specifications with change due in September 2017. In the 'Draft proposals for GCSE consultation 2016' from the Council for Curriculum, Examinations and Assessment (CCEA) – there is the following quote:

> Awarding Bodies are revising their GCSE and GCE speci-fications to ensure that both content and assessment continue to reflect the needs of learners and the society, economy and environment in which they live and work.[14]

From September 2017, there is a planned GCSE and GCE in Digital Technology for Northern Ireland. It is worth noting that schools in Northern Ireland also use English-based awarding bodies such as the Oxford, Cambridge and RSA Examinations (OCR). The best advice available to keep up-to-date is to keep checking with the council for the Curriculum Examinations and Assessment (CEA) for any notices regarding changes to the curriculum and with CAS Northern Ireland.

Scotland

The curriculum in Scotland is also being redesigned. For quite a few years, Scotland has been investing in and supporting Scotland's Digital Future. Behind the changes to the Scottish curriculum are PLAN C (Professional Learning and Networking in Computing). Figure 1.7 shows phase 1 of PLAN C, which shows a structured plan of developing teachers and learners.

Figure 1.7 Computing in Scotland

- A programme focusing on Pedagogical Content Knowledge for effective teaching of the new senior phase Computing Science qualifications that develops deep understanding and secure progression to further study in STEM and other disciplines.

- A programme focusing on developing Computational Thinking in the broad general education phase for Primary and Secondary teachers in the technologies curricular area.

- A programme focusing on advanced concepts and techniques in the senior phase to give teachers a greater understanding of the next step in our learners' journeys.

Sources: www.cas.scot/plan-c/ and
http://academy.bcs.org/content/computing-scottish-schools

For up-to-date relevant information, it is advisable to follow CAS Scotland online.

Now that we have explored the United Kingdom, we will look at the similarities and differences between the education systems or curriculums – Table 1.1.

United States of America

Having looked at the UK, we now 'look across the pond' to one of the world's leading countries – the USA – to see how they manage a computing curriculum.

In 2016, President Obama announced a 'Computer Science for All'[15] initiative for all pupils from kindergarten to high school; however, the teaching of computer science in the USA is non-compulsory and individual education districts set their own curriculum. While at state level computer science is recognised, at district level, individual districts choose what happens.

13

Table 1.1 Education system comparison in the UK

	England	Wales	Scotland	Northern Ireland
Awarding bodies	Many awarding bodies – such as OCR and the Assessment and Qualifications Alliance (AQA)	Many awarding bodies – such as the Welsh Joint Education Committee (WJEC)/ Eduqas, OCR and AQA (all approved by Qualifications Wales)	One awarding body – Scottish Qualifications Authority	CCEA – Council for Curriculum, Examinations and Assessment
Types of schools	Academies, free schools, state schools, grammar schools, faith schools, city technology colleges, private schools, state boarding schools	Maintained state schools. No academies, free schools, state schools or grammar schools	Education authority schools – local schools and special schools, denominational schools, Gaelic education, independent schools	Maintained schools, controlled schools,[15] integrated schools, independent schools Irish Medium Further Education (FE) Colleges
Language	English	Welsh (Cymraeg) is compulsory in schools as a first or second language English	Scottish Gaelic Medium is used in some schools English	Irish Medium is used in some schools English

(Continued)

Table 1.1 (Continued)

	England	Wales	Scotland	Northern Ireland
National curriculum	There is a national curriculum which is followed by most schools	There will be a curriculum for Wales – set for launch in September 2018	There is a Scottish Curriculum for Excellence	There is a UICT curriculum which all pupils up to end of KS4 must have the opportunity to follow
Teaching council	National College for Teaching and Leadership	There is the General Teaching Council for Wales (GTCW)	There is a General Teaching Council for Scotland	General Teaching Council Northern Ireland (GTCNI)
Subjects	A full range of subjects is taught including computing/ computer science	A full range of subjects is taught including computing/ computer science	A full range of subjects is taught including computing/ computer science	A full range of subjects is taught including computing/ computer science
Terminology (1)	The term National Curriculum is used	The term National Curriculum is used	The term Scotland Curriculum for Excellence is used	The term Northern Ireland Curriculum is used

(Continued)

Table 1.1 (Continued)

	England	Wales	Scotland	Northern Ireland
Terminology (2)	Reception is for ages 4–5	Reception is for ages 4–5	Pupils have seven years of primary school, starting in P1, equivalent to England year 1 and going through to P7	Foundation stage is ages 4–5. The term key stage is used. Key stage 1 is ages 6–7 and key stage 2 is ages 8–11
Primary	The term 'key stage' is used. Key stage 1 covers year 1 and year 2, ages 5–7. Key stage 2 covers years 3–6, ages 7–11	The term 'key stage' is used. Key stage 1 covers year 1 and year 2, ages 5–7. Key stage 2 covers years 3–6, ages 7–11		
Terminology (3)	The term 'key stage' is used. 'Key stage 3 and 4' covers secondary education. Secondary education starts at age 11–12 (year 7)	The term 'key stage' is used. 'Key stage 3 and 4' covers secondary education. Secondary education starts at age 11–12 (year 7)	Six years of secondary school. The term 'key stage' is not used. Secondary education starts at S1, equivalent to year 8 in England	The term 'key stage' is used. 'Key stage 3 and 4' covers secondary education up to the age of 16. Secondary education starts at age 11–12 (year 8)
Secondary				

(Continued)

Table 1.1 (Continued)

	England	Wales	Scotland	Northern Ireland
Terminology (4) Secondary/ 6th Form	The term key stage 5 is used for education after GCSEs, between the ages of 16–18. This is also called years 12 and 13	After key stage 4, year 12, pupils can enter years 13 and 14	After compulsory schooling, pupils can enter S5 and S6, equivalent to English years 12 and 13	After GCSEs, pupils can enter years 13 and 14
GCSEs	At age 15 to 16 pupils sit exams called GCSEs	At age 15 to 16 pupils sit exams called GCSEs	At the age of 15 to 16 pupils sit exams called Scotland National 4+5. This is the Scottish equivalent of a GCSE taken at the end of S4	At age 15 to 16 pupils sit exams called GCSEs
Vocational qualifications	There are vocational qualifications offered at age 15 to 16	There are vocational qualifications offered at age 15 to 16	There are Scottish Vocational Qualifications offered at age 15 to 16	There are vocational qualifications offered at age15 to 16
Age 15 to 16	Must continue education in some format after GCSEs	End of compulsory schooling	End of compulsory schooling	Must continue education in some format after GCSEs

Research carried out by Michael Jones of the University of Kent notes a few key points as shown in Figure 1.8.

Figure 1.8 School education in the USA

In the USA there are in excess of 14,000 school districts. Each of these has a degree of autonomy over what must be taught and what may be taught. Each State has an education board which provides some guidance and some mandate to districts. Districts largely decide on their education policy. This is an exemplar *par excellence* on devolving power locally. Colorado for example has a total of 179 school districts. Numbers are uneven, with the largest district, Denver, having a school population of approximately 88,000 and Agate having a population of 33. It is perhaps surprising that there is very little in the way of mandating at a Federal level. The picture in the USA is one where States do not have to adopt national standards. This is evidenced through the adherence to the new Common Core Standards. The Standards are a set of attainment rubrics in English, arts and mathematics designed to ensure commonality across the nation.

In England, the National Curriculum for every child is decided and, assuming it passes into law, each school district and thereby state-funded school is required to follow it, almost all. Academies have the right to not teach the National Curriculum.

Source: www.wcmt.org.uk/sites/default/files/report-documents/Jones%20 M%20Report%202015%20%20Final.pdf

Due to the lack of a non-compulsory curriculum at key stage 3 and 4, it is difficult to make a direct comparison. However, some comparisons are made in Table 1.2 to illustrate some of the differences between the English and American approach to implementing and teaching computer science.

Table 1.2 England vs USA curriculum comparison

	England	USA
Subject association	Non-government organisation (Computing At School – CAS) influential in advising on the new Computing curriculum	Non-government organisation (Computer Science Teachers Association – CSTA) influential in supporting and promoting the teaching of computer science
Subject association sponsorship	CAS is sponsored by commercial organisations	CSTA is sponsored by commercial organisations
Terminology 1	Key stage 3 (years 7–9)	Grades 6–8
Terminology 2	Key stage 4 (years 10 and 11)	Grades 9 and 10
Terminology 3	Key stage 5 (years 12 and 13)	Grades 11 and 12
Formal exams 1	GCSEs	No GCSE equivalent
Formal exams 2	A-level with new A-level specifications for first teaching from September 2015	Advanced principles certificate in computer science
A-level comparison	Assessment weighted with formal examinations (80%) and a programming project of 20%	Reverse situation, with greater emphasis on project-based assessment and less emphasis on the use of Java as a programming language

(Continued)

Table 1.2 (Continued)

	England	USA
Cross-curricular links	No formal mapping of strands across other areas of study • **(this point is developed in Chapter 3)**	No formal mapping across other subject areas but **'cross walks'** are encouraged to other subject areas
Resources	Some emphasis on partnership working. Massive Open Online Courses (MOOCs[17]), are not widely used	Greater emphasis on partnership working at higher levels to help address the teacher skills shortage. Also MOOCs are being used as a way of managing the teacher shortage

From this comparison, you can see that countries are adapting to move with the digital world.

To conclude this section, it is worth noting the following quotes.

> We are teaching children for jobs that don't exist. So, everything has to be about building resilience, problem solving and collaboration.
>
> Kathie Drake
> Primary Computing Co-ordinator and Year 2 teacher

This quote is extremely relevant. Only a few examples are included in this chapter but across the world there is investment in education to ensure that the next generation is fully equipped with the correct skills for a newly emerging job market.

> My most satisfied moments in teaching are what I call GOTCHA Moments when a student makes a connection or "gets" an idea.
>
> Chris Sharples
> Head of Computing (Secondary)

This quote is food for thought – countries are asking how they can enable every single pupil to achieve such GOTCHA moments in computer science; developing their knowledge and skills in the age of digitalisation. This is certainly an extremely exciting time in computing education as you can see across the UK and the USA. Enjoy being a part of a major change in education!

2 THE ROLE OF THE COMPUTER SCIENCE TEACHER

In this chapter we will examine what the role of a computer science teacher encompasses, discuss the responsibilities of a teacher and analyse attributes, knowledge and skills used in a teaching role. There will be a focus on job adverts and titles, along with advice on securing a teaching role.

INTRODUCTION TO THE ROLE

Consider the quote by Steven Gibson, a Primary Computing Co-ordinator, Year 5 teacher, CAS Master Teacher and CAS Hub Leader.

> Teaching is all about verbalising passion to make the lesson contagious.

This is what the computer science teacher does in the classroom. Think of the role of the computer science teacher as opening the gateway for pupils to grasp or interact and become fully immersed in the technological age. See yourself as a moulder of minds who may go on to create innovation that will benefit society. Even if the pupils in front of you do not go on to create the latest cutting edge technology, you are giving them the knowledge, skills and understanding to operate comfortably and safely in the world in which they interact. Running alongside imparting skills and knowledge to pupils is mentoring, coaching and supporting a young person through their experience of education. More on this is discussed in the section on attributes, knowledge and skills needed by a teacher in this chapter.

At this point it is worth noting that as a computer science teacher, you won't always be teaching to a GCSE specification; there are other types of courses available at key stage 4 and 5, such as Pearson Business and Technology Education Council (BTEC) qualifications. The BTEC qualification is vocational as opposed to a GCSE, which is a traditional pathway, and examined differently. Additionally, you may find yourself in the decision process of what qualifications to offer at key stage 4 as an alternative to a GCSE. The list of approved qualifications can change from year to year, so before deciding on which qualifications to offer, you need to check the gov.uk website for approved qualifications.

Responsibilities

Starting on the premise that teaching is all about passion, we will start to look at some of the realities of teaching life. The classroom is not an isolated experience. It requires the teacher to have additional responsibilities beyond it. Every computer science teacher will have responsibilities both in and out of the classroom some of which are shown in Table 2.1.

Table 2.1 Responsibilities in and out of the classroom

Responsibilities IN the classroom	Responsibilities OUT of the classroom
Planning and preparing, delivering lessons	Promoting the subject through attendance at:
	Parents' evenings
	Open evenings
	Options evenings

(Continued)

Table 2.1 (Continued)

Responsibilities IN the classroom	Responsibilities OUT of the classroom
Monitoring pupil progress	Attending whole-school staff meetings
Ensuring pupils are geared towards learning and providing a safe learning environment	Ensuring the school in general is a safe environment for young people
Setting homework	Attending departmental staff meetings
Marking pupil work – class and homework	• Teachers with additional responsibilities will be involved in writing departmental self-reviews to feed into school development plans
Planning engaging wall displays for the classrooms	• Teachers with additional responsibilities will also manage other staff
Duty of Care to all pupils	

Additionally, teachers will interact with others such as teaching colleagues, parents and outside agencies.[18]

Many new secondary teachers find themselves being a form tutor (the primary equivalent of this is your class that you teach all the time for one year and then change). This may be to a group of around 20 to 30 pupils, who you would see at least once per day and be the provider of their pastoral support.[19] As a form tutor, you will be the first point of their support system for that group of pupils for their entire life at secondary school, for example, from year 7 (age 11 to 12) through to year 11 (age 15 to 16).

Some of the things that a form tutor does with a tutor group are:

- checks that they have the correct equipment – pens, pencils, rulers, physical education (PE) kit and anything else to make the school day successful;

- liaises with parents or carers;

- liaises with the school's child protection or safeguarding team;

- liaises with the head of year group, exams officers, School Medical Officer, head teacher and members of the senior leadership team;

- supports pupils in forming friendships within the tutor group;

- checks that homework is completed;

- checks that planners[20] are signed. Note that some schools have started to introduce digital planners. Speak with your school for the system in place for checking on parental engagement with a planner.

As a form tutor you will find yourself dealing with pupils who may have either social or pastoral issues, examples of which can include leaving the house without breakfast on a regular basis; not eating every day; arriving to school without the correct equipment for a successful day, such as pens, textbooks, exercise books, uniform, shoes or PE kit; unstable and turbulent home lives including violence and varying forms of abuse; being a carer for a family member; poor hygiene such as lice, body odour; poor attendance and sudden changes in behaviour. As a form tutor you may be the first person that notices these matters. Concerns should always be referred to the school's safeguarding team in writing and followed up in person. Once this is done, follow the advice provided on the best way forward in dealing with the matter.

Essentially, as a class teacher and a form tutor, you are working under the heading **'Help Children Achieve More'** to ensure that every child is healthy, safe, enjoying school, making positive contributions to school life and is set up to achieve economic well-being.

The following quote gives an insight into one teacher's realisation during her early days of tutelage.

> I wish I had realised how many pupils come from a difficult or challenging background. I was unprepared for the number of pupils for whom education is not the priority.
> Jayne Fenton-Hall
> Head of IT and Computing (Secondary)

Being a form tutor or a teacher and coming across either social or pastoral issues can be a very sobering experience. Many of your pupils will not come from the same background as you and a high level of adaptability and empathy are required on your part to manage all within the pupil population. One needs to think of the impact that these issues have on the individual pupil and the effect the issues have on what you are trying to get them to achieve in the classroom. These issues have a massive impact upon pupil progress and attainment.

ATTRIBUTES, KNOWLEDGE AND SKILLS

In this subsection, the attributes, knowledge and skills required to be a successful computer science teacher are addressed. These lists are not exhaustive but give an indication of what is required. At the start of one's career a teacher may not possess all the skills and most certainly many will be in development. This is the purpose of the Newly Qualified Teacher (NQT) Year. Even for an established teacher, many skills will be ongoing development.

Having read each section, take the self-assessments in Appendix 1 and mark yourself against the attributes, knowledge and skills. In education, there is a constant state of professional development and at no stage in your career will you have learnt 'everything' you will ever need to know on every front.

Attributes

The **attributes** required by all teachers are those of:

- **Organisation and preparation** – these attributes cannot be stressed strongly enough. In a teaching day, this means that you know what materials are required for each of the lessons you will teaching, be this from computers, materials for unplugged activities,[21] the register, books, pens, pencils, rulers, boxes of tissues for runny noses, a seating plan (an example is given in Appendix 2) with names of pupils and notes about any of their needs to help you to manage the learning environment – your classroom. You need to know everything you can about your classroom and learners. This attribute is summed up in the following quote.

Organisation is affective and effective.[22]

- **Reflection** – throughout your teaching career, it is recommended to be a reflective practitioner and after each lesson, day, week, topic, it is worth looking at what went well (**www**) and what would be even... better...if... (**ebi**). This attribute allows you to develop into a strong and outstanding teacher. By using reflective techniques, you will refine your practice and be able to see how teaching the same topic to pupils of differing abilities, genders and social circumstances may need to be adapted. Another scenario in which it is useful is knowing how groups of pupils behave at different times of the day: first lesson of the day, before break time, before lunch, after lunch, last lesson of the day. This is useful in helping you to plan what topics you will introduce or teach and knowing how to get the best out of your audience. Being a reflective practitioner is vital.

- **Listening** – at many times, to gain an understanding of the learning environment you may need to take a step back and listen. This means listening to the way in which the pupils see the subject, listen to what they enjoy, what is not working as well, what they would like to still learn, and where have they applied the knowledge and skills you have taught them. Listening helps to inform your practice.

- **Empathy** – with many activities in the classroom, such as unplugged activities, paired programming (covered in Chapter 3) and class discussion, pupils will have different ideas; some will understand a concept quicker and pupils may get frustrated with each other, thus there may be a need to diffuse conflict. This is the social and moral part of the job, where teachers and pupils must learn to respect each other's opinions and differences. In teaching you will frequently hear the term 'Spiritual, Moral, Social and Cultural' (SMSC).[23] This is not only for pupils but a rule of thumb for the whole school community.

- **Curiosity** – within the new curriculum, curiosity is highly encouraged at pupil level. It is also an attribute required by the teacher – especially in a subject which is fast changing. This does not mean being skilled and well versed in the next big program or device, but it means being aware of what is happening. A great way of doing this is by reading computing and technology news. Within the classroom, encourage pupils during extension activities to seek further information on a computing topic in the news or perhaps in a starter activity to discuss the points raised in a news piece.

- **Respectful** – when managing the classroom with many different individuals, you will encounter pupils from a range of backgrounds and every single one with a different opinion. As a teacher, we are never to judge and most definitely not to give our opinion on pupils or other members of staff or to decide one product is better over another based upon our likes or dislikes. Discussions

THE ROLE OF THE COMPUTER SCIENCE TEACHER

with pupils must be well balanced. This is another element of the SMSC aspect of the teaching role.

- **Authoritative** – the class always needs to know who is in charge and what is permissible within the learning and school environments. As an educator, you should always celebrate the positive within the classroom and issue rewards if appropriate, and when expectations are not met or school rules are not followed then the classroom and organisation sanctions policy must be followed. Ensuring that these two are working in harmony will help you in establishing your authority within the classroom.

- **Cross-curricular thinker** – the teacher with the curious mind will also see links with other subjects. This helps when speaking to your pupils as you will always be able to take them beyond your classroom and show them the power of the subject in a wider sense. It is wise to be aware of what is going on in other subject areas and how a link can be forged with computing. In the 'promoting your subject' section in Chapter 3 of this book, some examples are offered on how this can be achieved.

- **Good communicator** – this goes without saying; a good to outstanding teacher will always be a good communicator, being able to give explanations and relay messages in a clear concise format and in language that is understood by the pupils. This means that if you are teaching a group of pupils who are challenged with understanding, you may need to further break down even the simplest steps. For example, some of you will come across pupils who are unable to relay a message home so the trick here is to write in their planner, so that the message is not misunderstood. Good communication also needs to be the case with your colleagues; everything must be clear and unambiguous. As a computer science teacher, you will recognise that ambiguity leads to poor solutions and outcomes!

- **Approachable** – this is essential in the classroom; you will have established leadership and authority. Pupils should feel safe in the classroom and will know that if there is an issue they can approach you and depending upon the problem, if it is a classroom issue such as being unable to see the interactive white board from a certain seat, you will be able to resolve the issue; or it may be a deeper problem, such as an issue within the year group or a group of pupils which needs to be referred on to the head of year or safeguarding team. Regardless of what the matter is, pupils should feel they can approach you, that you will listen, empathise and support them during their school journey.

Knowledge

The **knowledge** required by all computer science teachers is that of:

- **Working knowledge of the curriculum or programme of study** – to be able to competently and confidently teach across the key stages in which you work, such as key stage 1 and 2 or 3 and key stage 4 or key stage 3–5. It goes without saying that in-depth subject knowledge is key. To ascertain if you have the right level of knowledge, a good starting point is a self-audit against the 'Subject knowledge requirements for entry into computer science teacher training' guide, published by the teaching agency.[24] Table 2.2 shows knowledge required at secondary level. To work out the requirements for primary level, look at the original document, say in the Algorithm strand for example, and A1–A6 will show the knowledge for primary level.

This is an excellent way of ascertaining where your Continuing Professional Development (CPD) needs lie. Would you be able to differentiate such activities for a weak ability versus a higher ability group? Having this level of knowledge is important in being able to deliver the curriculum successfully.

Table 2.2 Subject knowledge requirements for entry into computer science teacher training

Range and content	Algorithms	Programming	Data	Computing and social informatics	Communication and the internet
In addition to the above, a student about to embark on secondary teacher training as a computer science specialist should know, understand and be able to:	A7 Explain how the choice of an algorithm should be influenced by the data. A8 Be able to explain and use several key algorithms (e.g. sorting, searching, shortest path).	P10 Program competently in at least two programming languages, at least one of which must be 'textual'. P11 Explain and use programming concepts such as selection, repetition, procedures, constants, variables, relational operators, logical operators and functions.	D6 Explain the difference between data and information. D7 Explain the need for and use of hexadecimal, two's complement, signed integers and string manipulation.	C9 Explain the use of logic gates and registers. C10 Explain Von Neumann architecture.	I6 Explain the concepts of: client/server models; MAC addresses, IP addresses and domain names; and cookies.

(Continued)

Table 2.2 (Continued)

Range and content	Algorithms	Programming	Data	Computing and social informatics	Communication and the internet
	A9 Explain how algorithms can be improved, validated, tested and corrected. A10 Explain that a single problem could be solved by more than one algorithm. A11 Explain and show how different algorithms can have different performance characteristics for the same task.	P12 Explain and use truth tables and Boolean valued variables. P13 Explain and use two-dimensional arrays (and higher). P14 Explain and use nested constructs (e.g. a loop that contains a conditional, and vice versa). P15 Explain the concept of procedures that call procedures.	D8 Explain the need for data compression, and be able to describe simple compression methods. D9 Explain the need for analogue to digital conversions and how this works. D10 Explain the limitations of using binary representations – e.g. rounding errors, sampling frequency and fractional numbers.	C11 Explain the fetch–execute cycle. C12 Explain and use low-level instruction sets and assembly code. C13 Explain what compilers and interpreters are and do and give some examples of when they are used.	I7 Explain a 'real protocol' e.g. using telnet to interact with an HTTP server. I8 Explain routing; redundancy and error correction; encryption and security.

Table 2.2 (Continued)

Range and content	Algorithms	Programming	Data	Computing and social informatics	Communication and the internet
	A12 Successfully apply algorithms in solving GCSE and A-level type problems.	P16 Explain how low-level languages work and when they are used, being able to give simple examples. P17 Explain that a program can be written to satisfy requirements and that they should be corrected if they do not meet these. P18 Successfully apply programming in solving computing/ computer science GCSE and A-level type problems.	D11 Explain how structured data can be represented in tables in a relational database, and simple database queries.	C14 Explain the main functions of operating systems.	

Note: MAC = Media Access Control; IP = Internet Protocol; HTTP = Hypertext Transfer Protocol.

Computer science teachers should also have a good awareness of what is happening in the wider industry. A good way of doing this is following computing and technology news, as previously mentioned. Currently some of the 'hot topics' in the computer industry are:

- Big Data and the Internet of Things (IoT);
- how computing/IT is changing fields such as medicine/the National Health Service (NHS);
- how computers have changed route planning/travel/ banking and how this trend is set to continue;
- cybersecurity;
- quantum computers;
- robotics;
- the impact of artificial intelligence (AI) and the impact of AI on autonomous systems.

Cognisance of what is happening in the industry helps to make class discussions impactful.

- **Working knowledge of at least one awarding body at key stages 4 and 5 (secondary teachers only)** – the school in which you teach will be following the specification set by an awarding body. The specification will state what needs to be taught at key stages 4 to 5 for pupils to be successful at GCSE or A-level. Some teachers may find themselves being the only teacher in the department and having to choose the awarding body for computer science. It is advisable to look at the following factors: weighting between formal examination and controlled assessment and the needs of the cohort, quality and quantity of support material and resources available from the awarding body – availability of textbooks, online support and customer service, teaching videos, sample schemes of work and past exam papers to support your delivery of a specification.

- **Understanding of prior key stages** – when teaching at any level, it is a good idea to have an appreciation of the previous key stage for computing, so that you are aware of what knowledge, skills and understanding pupils should have gained before arriving at your school and into your class. This will also help you when explaining concepts and moving pupil knowledge on, as you will be able to provide the 'hook', and refer to pupil's prior knowledge and experience. For example, in year 7 if you are going to teach flowcharting and Pseudocode, you will recap algorithms, you may wish to ask pupils about using Beebots[25] in the classroom at primary school and to explain what they did with the Beebots and how they worked. Then the lesson can be taken further by looking at how algorithms can be represented through flowcharts, then onto Pseudocode. In this way, you are not re-teaching a topic but are instead building upon pre-existing knowledge and prior experience. Even if a pupil has not been taught the word 'algorithm' at key stage 2, you can link into other activities they would have done such as 'the Christmas play'; in this example you can ask pupils to recall the instructions or sequences and decisions they made on the stage during the Christmas play: these are all examples of algorithms.

  The school in which you work generally has one or more feeder[26] schools. It is advisable to visit the feeder schools to meet the teachers and pupils to see their computer science journey, as this will greatly help you in your teaching. Some schools host their local feeder schools for a computing day and this is also a good way of making links and improving your overall knowledge. The same concept applies to a primary school working with their feeder pre-school.

- **Understanding of onward key stages** – knowing the onward journey is essential, as in the classroom you will be able to explain to pupils how a topic links to further study; for example when teaching logic gates at secondary level, you will be able to explain to pupils that at key stage 5, this ground knowledge will be used for learning about simplification of Boolean expressions using Karnaugh maps and DeMorgans law, and that a practical application of Karnaugh maps is in recognising patterns and pattern recognition. This will show pupils that there is relevance of the topic beyond the classroom. In this example, you won't be teaching Karnaugh maps but simply have an appreciation of what comes next.

A good way for you to understand the onward journey for your pupils is to visit colleges and sixth forms in the local area which your pupils may go to (if your school does not go beyond key stage 4). Some colleges also host their local schools and again this is another way of understanding links across key stages. Again, the same concept applies to a primary teacher appreciating the transition to secondary. If such links do not exist it is wise to forge these bonds for the greater good of computing education and your teaching practice.

- **Diversity within computing** – understanding the needs of the pupils in the classroom will help you to get the most out of the pupils and ensure that each pupil achieves their full potential. This involves being aware of factors such as gender differences, issues that may affect different ethnic groups, Special Education Needs (SEN) pupils, different socio-economic groups, and so on. As a teacher, you will also need to be aware of the language that you use within the school environment so that there is no leaning towards 'unconscious bias'. Additionally, awareness of national initiatives to promote and combat issues around diversity is necessary. This will be explored further in the 'Diversity and inclusion in the computing classroom' section in Chapter 3.

- **Working knowledge of the teacher's standards**[27] – these outline the minimum expectations of every teacher with qualified teacher status (QTS) or every trainee teacher working towards achieving QTS. While this is not subject specific, it is profession specific and adherence is required. As an educator, you are accountable for ensuring that the highest standards of work and conduct are maintained at all times. There is more discussion on this area in the 'Standards' section in Chapter 3 of this book.

- **Working knowledge of the BCS Certificate in Computer Science Teaching** – this is a professionally recognised certificate that is designed to complement academic qualifications. The certificate requires the teacher to:

  1. Attend and participate in professional development activities within the community such as CAS Hubs and other relevant CPD such as online training.

  2. Demonstration of subject knowledge skills, such as through a programming project which can be directly applied to classroom practice.

  3. Demonstration of an investigative approach to the pedagogy of computer science, such as through unplugged activities, pair programming, group work and so on.

- **Technical skills** – in addition to good subject knowledge, a computer science teacher should have wider technical skills, for example, a familiarity with the inside workings and internals of a computer. It is advisable to know what is inside the computer case and not to approach this as a purely theoretical subject. (Note that it is not necessary to be able to build computers or be a computer engineer but to just have an awareness. The course specification that you deliver will give guidance on what level of technical knowledge or skill is required.) For example, when teaching on logic gates, it will help to show pupils a Central Processing Unit (CPU)[28] and identify transistors on the CPU and explain that this is one example of where the knowledge they are gaining is used. This will allow for a spiritual moment of SMSC in your lesson. Usually a 'wow' moment for pupils.

- **The school values and vision** – each school has a School Development Plan (SDP), which outlines what the school wishes to achieve over a certain time frame. As a subject specialist, you need to know how your subject feeds into the SDP; for example, a school may have points of focus such as increased participation in enrichment activities, raising attainment for pupils within the pupil premium category,[29] or raising attainment for girls or boys in certain subject areas, removing barriers to learning such as by having computer suites open at lunch times and after school so that pupils without computers at home can use the facilities, or looking at ways of encouraging independent learners.

- **How the school fits within the community** – knowing how your school compares with other schools in the vicinity and their offerings is powerful; this will come into play at events like open evenings[30] and options evenings[31] where parents and other visitors come to the school and you will usually have a central role in promoting the subject and encouraging pupils to join the school and study your subject. Selling points such as your school being a lead school in the CAS Network of Excellence (NoE) or being a CAS Hub will greatly help in how the school is seen within the community.

- **Understanding of other subjects and departments** – being aware of common language used across subjects will greatly enhance your teaching; for example, the term variable is used when teaching the sciences; if at secondary, find out from the science teachers when, where and how this term is used and then draw links with computer science. A primary teacher should have the awareness and pull the terms across topics when teaching. Another example of awareness is knowing which other subjects use pattern recognition, such as art, and drawing on them in your lessons. Again this will help you to be that outstanding teacher. There will be more on this in the 'Techniques' section of this book in Chapter 3.

- **Understanding of local and national initiatives for the subject and for education in general** – an outstanding teacher always sees beyond the classroom; as such, you should be aware of enrichment activities in which your pupils can take part at local, national and international levels. One way of doing this is linking up with your local Science, Technology, Engineering, Mathematics (STEM) or Science, Technology, Engineering, Arts, Mathematics (STEAM) group who will be aware of these activities. Reading technology press, education news, the CAS website and CAS newsletters is also beneficial as it will keep you up-to-date with what is occurring in Computing education.

Skills

This section will look at subject-specific skills and general skills which when combined will help you to develop excellent practise in the computing classroom.

Subject-specific skills

We will now look at subject-related skills, which are those specific to the computer science teacher. Central to your role as a subject specialist is teaching CT.[32]

> Computational thinking is the thought processes involved in formulating a problem and expressing its solution(s) in such a way that a computer – human or machine – can effectively carry out.
>
> Jeannette M. Wing

This is, in essence, problem solving and provides the structure for the subject. You are enabling pupils to be able to solve problems through devising solutions. This requires pupils to consider different conditions and to work alongside others to create the solution; as a computer science teacher, you are also enabling pupils to gain teamworking skills.

CT encompasses the following strands:

- **Abstraction** – this is where only the detail that is necessary to the functioning of the system is required. For example, in mapping flight routes across Europe, we are not interested in the countries below, land formations or any other detail; instead we are interested simply in a route from, say London to Madrid or Lisbon, Reykjavik. The thick black lines in Figure 2.1 serve to illustrate this point.

Figure 2.1 Map of Europe showing flights between capital cities

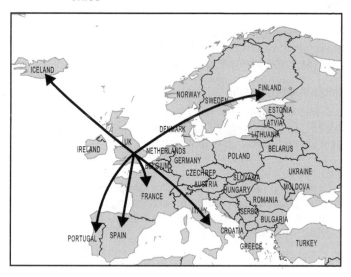

- **Algorithm design** – the purpose of an algorithm is to show the definitive steps in solving a problem. Algorithms are all around us and are not specific to computer science. In fact, your pupils will be using algorithms every day, from making cupcakes in a catering lesson, to experiments in science. Most would have been captivated by magic tricks[33] at some point in their lives – another example of algorithmic thinking. Algorithms can be expressed in a variety ways, such as drawn as a flowchart or written in Pseudocode.

- **Decomposition** – involves looking at a problem and then solving it by breaking it down into smaller parts. Each part is then solved and when put back together will solve the initial bigger problem. Decomposing a problem allows for a quicker solution and debugging. For example, if a pupil is presented with a fruit salad, and asked how to make it, they would need to decompose it into the parts of the fruit salad, such as apples, pears, oranges, grapes, and so on, and then further break this down by having to wash and chop these fruits. This can be further refined into how the fruit should be chopped – into cubes, longitudinally, and so on. Once these details are worked through then all parts are put together and a fruit salad is made.

- **Pattern recognition** – involves looking at sets of data and spotting patterns and trends, from which one can then make a prediction or draw a conclusion. For example, this could be applied when analysing handwriting, looking at angles of the writing, forward or backward slants, heavy imprint or lighter writing. Based upon the patterns identified, conclusions as to what a person's personality is may be drawn. Other examples of pattern recognition can be seen in repetitive dance steps in dances like the Macarena or the 'cha cha slide'. Being able to spot patterns then helps the programmer to program the computer to carry out complex tasks efficiently.

- **Generalisation** – is closely linked to pattern recognition and is sometimes referred to as pattern generalisation. An example of this can be seen when reading a story; for example, looking for nouns that appear will let you recognise that objects are being discussed, or looking for verbs that appear will let you know that an action is occurring. Generalisation can also be explained as focusing on refining the solution to present a generalised solution for all cases.

- **Evaluation** – when evaluating a solution, we need to ensure that the solution solves the initial problem given. This can be done through testing and using a test plan, looking at what is expected and what actually happens, along with finer points such as user friendliness of the solution and efficiency.

At this point it is encouraged to undertake further reading or viewing on CT through the following means:

- Kemp, P. (2014) *Computing in the National Curriculum – A Guide for Secondary Teachers.* Computing at School (CAS).

- Berry, M. (2013) *Computing in the National Curriculum – A Guide for Primary Teachers.* Computing at School (CAS).

- BBC Bitesize Computational Thinking Videos – for primary and secondary (Appendix 8).

- Beecher, K. (2017) *Computational Thinking – A Beginner's Guide to Problem Solving and Programming.* BCS Learning and Development Ltd, Swindon – for GCSE, A-level.

It is also worth noting that in the classroom one should familiarise themselves with a range of unplugged activities to teach the various concepts of CT. At primary level, there are the CAS Barefoot resources (which are also suitable for explaining concepts at secondary) and for secondary there is the CAS Tenderfoot project. Both develop the basics of CT and give teachers further in-depth subject knowledge.

The benefit of using unplugged activities is that they get pupils thinking about the actual process they are following; thus, you are teaching them to problem solve. It is essential that computer science teachers do not approach the subject as 'programming'; there are different elements to computer science and great problem solvers create great innovations. To further clarify this point, think about the English language; we know the structure of a sentence: beginning, middle, end. We recognise verbs, nouns and adjectives. This same principle is applied across all languages. However, to learn specifically how to speak another language then you undertake training or lessons in that language. The same is to be said for computer science; we learn the problem solving and then it can be shown through programming in a variety of different languages. Remember that not every pupil is or would like to be a programmer, but all should have the opportunity to learn how to program.

General skills

We will now address general skills required by teachers. Some of these are:

- **Leadership** – quite simply put, your class needs to know that you are in charge. Pupils like and need guidance, direction and routine, they need to know that you are the teacher and that the journey you will take them on in the computing classroom will lead to a series of end goals. Show the class the power of the subject beyond the classroom walls. The class also needs to know your expectations of them. Always state these to each new class and with some classes these will need to be repeated many times.

- **Problem solver** – here we are not talking about CT. That has already been covered. What this is about is being a multi-tasker, having the ability to manage a variety of situations in the classroom at the same time and the ability to think on one's feet and to make decisions quickly. Additionally, you need to be able to diffuse and resolve conflict quickly; for example, as a teacher you may be on a contractual break duty and there is a group of pupils perhaps having an argument or involved in a playground 'scrap'; you will need to be able to disperse the pupils before the situation becomes a bigger and more serious matter **(note a teacher is never to go wading into any form of affray)**. Usually these situations can be dissolved with humour. Another way in which problem solving comes into play on a regular basis is when colleagues are absent and a supply teacher[34] is recruited to cover the absent colleague's teaching – sometimes this occurs at short notice. As a permanent member of staff, you may find yourself having to plan and set cover work and supporting the supply teacher in addition to your own workload. Teaching involves spinning a lot of plates at the same time.

- **Ability to maintain good relationships with other staff, pupils and parents** – a teacher cannot exist in isolation and hope to be successful. This is a profession that relies heavily on interpersonal and networking skills. At a basic level, your main interactions will be with pupils, other colleagues and parents. Pupil interaction occurs on a minute by minute, hour to hour, day to day basis, term to term, year to year. It is vital to have good rapport with pupils, to make your life easier and to ensure they have a positive schooling experience. This does not mean that you are 'friends' with your pupils, rather that you are aware of how to get the best out of every pupil, for example, through motivating them. Knowing the likes and dislikes of your pupils is a winner. Every computer science teacher at some point will be greeted by the pupil who arrives at the classroom door and declares that they 'hate computer science!' or they 'hate computing!'. It is always worthwhile finding out the hobbies and interest of your class, and being able to relate what is being taught to their interest; this will raise levels of engagement within the classroom.

Pupils are one dimension, good relationships with your colleagues must never be underestimated as colleagues across the school at all levels in the school hierarchy are your allies and support network. Knowing what is going on in other departments and seeking ways for cross-curricular links, such as joint subject assemblies and joint enrichment activities, helps to cement relationships with other staff. Attending staff social events is also another important way of interacting with staff across the school, for example, when going to the Christmas party or other social event such as bowling night, termly meal out, and so on. It's worth sitting on a table with colleagues from a different year group or department. A simple act such as this allows you to speak with colleagues in a different setting and reaps rewards when you are back in the work environment.

The third part of the dimension is maintaining good relationships with parents. Keeping parents informed of positive and negative matters is important and positives need to be celebrated with postcards home, notes in planners or through the relevant system the school uses to communicate with parents. The same is to be said for negative matters, through phone calls home, letters or meeting the parent (with another colleague present). Parent evenings are another opportunity to interact with parents, however, these should be positive experiences and if there is a matter that requires urgent attention, it should be dealt with long before a parents' evening.

As one progresses further in their career, your professional community becomes wider and will include others such as school governors and on occasion, outside agencies, such as educational psychologists and school health teams. If you are a new entrant into the computer science teaching profession, being a member of a CAS Hub is a great way of interacting with others outside of your school and developing interpersonal skills. For example, giving a short presentation at a local hub meeting on a topic such as sharing good practice and sharing your classroom successes is a good starting point.

Remember, teaching is a people-centred job! The business of teaching covers communication, negotiation and relating to others.

- **Enthuse, inspire, influence** – as a teacher, you will be a constant in the life of the pupils and your words and actions will have a great impact on shaping their futures, you are influential! As an educator, it is a part of your role to show pupils what they can become; this does not necessarily mean they must work in computing, rather that they can achieve greatness, and that computer science can be a part of that journey and how. A useful tool is to share your journey into teaching with pupils through assemblies; this can be at an options assembly when recruiting pupils to take up computer science at key stage 4 and 5,[35] or it can be a part of a careers assembly, careers day or first introduction to you at either primary or secondary level. Another way is to have a 'Teacher hall of fame', which shows the teachers, their journeys into teaching and their interests. Further ways of inspiring pupils are to have wall displays around the faculty or department area, on topics like influential women in digital technology, people with disabilities doing great work in computing, people of different ethnic origins achieving in computing, technological advances or news stories of the week, great inventions, jobs with direct and indirect links to computer science and many more.

- **Celebrate achievement** – as part of the job of enthusing, inspiring and influencing pupils we need to celebrate the positive. Find the positive in every day, every lesson, every term and every year! For the pupils, this translates into smiley faces in books or on a wall in the classroom, digital badges, computing champion badges worn on blazers, articles in the school newsletter, for example. This allows computing within your school to move beyond the classroom.

The amazing thing about celebrating the positive is that it makes you as the teacher feel a great sense of achievement and this radiates to your colleagues, making for a comfortable and rewarding working environment. Of course it also makes for a positive environment for all pupils. The skill here is to continually seek, identify and celebrate the positive! See the following quote.

Celebrate the positive in every day. It is always there, even when we have to look harder on some days.

- **Budget management** – many teachers think about the classroom element of the job; however, depending on whether you are a one-person department or a head of department or part of a department, there is a requirement to be aware of the budget allocation. Careful budget management is required in order that the pupils and teachers have the correct materials to ensure that the learning experience is positive. Examples of items which are sourced from the budget are exercise books, textbooks, marker pens, pencils, paper, mini white boards, printing costs, devices for physical computing such as Raspberry Pi's, subscriptions to online services, and so on. Budget size tends to vary greatly amongst schools and it is always worth knowing what the departmental budget covers and which budget covers items that are in every classroom such as Interactive White Boards (IWB).

- **Advise** – the skill here is to provide professional information and not to let your personal opinions creep in. As a teacher, pupils and colleagues will ask for your advice, for instance, on whether they should choose computer science as a subject to study at GCSE; this needs to be weighed up against factors such as the pupil's strengths, areas for development, career options and not whether they like the teacher or you like them, or simply to recruit more numbers to your subject. This will happen naturally if the information is presented unbiased. On occasion, your opinion may be sought by colleagues or senior leadership on matters such as best resources to buy in or awarding body choice – again, this information should be presented in a factual manner.

- **Adaptability** – during the course of a teaching day, week, month and year, a teacher finds themselves having to manage a variety of situations frequently at the very last minute. One such case could be finding out very late on that a room change is required for reasons beyond your control; although this is rare, this will mean having to move your class to a temporary room and deal with factors such as a slightly different seating plan and pupils being very excited or sometimes unhappy about being in a different room.

On a teaching level, adaptability is required when teaching a range of differing abilities from high ability to weak ability pupils; while training, all teachers would have learnt, practised and developed differentiation skills. In the classroom, differentiation is an ongoing skill and makes the difference in getting the most out of your learners. The needs of learners change from cohort to cohort and so too does the requirement to differentiate and personalise the learning experience.

Other ways in which a teacher may have to adapt is at secondary level – they may be required to change the awarding body which they have used for a few years; although this is rare it does happen and it may occur for an assortment of reasons. An awarding body change will require the teacher to understand fundamentals such as administration requirements of the new awarding body and course structure. Adaptability is summed up in the following phrase.

Responding to change is a basic teacher skill.

- **Patience** – this may not seem an obvious skill in this profession, however, it links closely with adaptability and differentiation. We need to think of the wide range of learners that a teacher encounters, all with varying needs. It is part of the teaching role to nurture a pupil who may find a computer science concept challenging. Progress varies greatly from one pupil to another. Within the computing classroom, to embed core concepts one great way is to have a raft of unplugged activities in your personal 'teacher toolkit'. This is important for explaining abstract concepts and ensuring that pupils can engage and understand before moving onto work on a computer. The patience factor here is finding the right words and resources that explain the topic.

- **Behaviour management** – this is specifically looking at how the teacher manages pupil behaviour; this is an ongoing skill and, as previously mentioned, it is important to set your expectations out to any pupils that you teach.

The correct behaviour must be present in the classroom to enable learning. While teachers have rewards and sanctions at their disposal, the most effective way of managing the classroom is to have the correct behaviour in place; this will translate most of the time to celebrating the positive and, on occasion, when there needs to be a sanction, that this is then effective.

Some examples of effective behaviour management strategies are:

- Ensure pupils have the correct equipment before entering the classroom, so that learning is the only thing occurring in the classroom.

- Ensure pupils are dressed properly in the room, not sitting in coats with poor or unkempt uniforms or listening to headphones and perhaps looking the other way while you speak to the class (less likely to happen at primary level).

- Ensure activities are structured and time bonded with an expectation of work completion.

- Set expectations on acceptable and appropriate behaviour in the learning environment.

- Use a range of activities and resources to engage pupils, some examples of which are individual work, paired work, group work, videos, Massive Open Online Courses (MOOCs), kinaesthetic activities, stand up, sit down activities, observe what is happening and report back activities, beat the clock activities, drawing as opposed to writing, and so on.

- Have a presence in the classroom, walk around as pupils are working, look at and read what they are doing, comment if necessary.

- Use strategies such as think, pair and share before getting responses from the class.

- Have a 'starter on arrival' activity for pupils to complete as soon as they enter the classroom, perhaps in relation to a topical news article.

- Excite pupils by telling them that you have looked forward to the lesson and tell them what you find exciting about the topic – this is part of you enthusing and influencing the lesson.

- Have a no hands up policy; this will avoid pupils 'hiding' and they will know that you can choose any pupil to answer questions.

- Use traffic light cards or emoji cards as another method to ascertain understanding, and if a pupil requires help during the main activity, there will be no need for them to call out, rather just to show their card without drawing attention to themselves or disrupting the group.

- Use questioning techniques such as questions directed to top pupils, weaker pupils, girls, boys, pupils with learning difficulties. Everyone should feel that they have something to contribute (this links into having a diverse and inclusive classroom).

- Further develop questioning by applying Blooms Taxonomy[36] of higher order questioning.

- Plenary activities should be structured so that pupils can say what they learnt, where they could use the lesson knowledge outside of school, where that knowledge could be used in school, how they would explain that knowledge to parents, younger children, the elderly, and so on.

- Reward pupils for contributing. On occasion, there may be a pupil who cannot participate in speaking, perhaps due to a social issue, however they can still take part in the classroom experience, for example, handing out or collecting in resources. Every pupil has a place in the classroom and a role to play! As an educator, it is part of your role to expect and get the best out of every pupil. Recall that at the start of this section, interpersonal skills were mentioned as being key; this is an area where they come into their own, when the teacher knows their learners.

- Non-verbal communication – you may remember from your own school days 'the teacher look': this means that when you look at your learners, and provide non-verbal cues, such as 'turn around', 'stop doing that', 'concentrate on your work' and so on, that the pupil knows exactly what is required, without you having to verbalise and possibly disrupt other pupils from working.

Included within behaviour management strategies is the use of assertive language as another key to discipline. For example, if a pupil is tapping a pen on the desk, you could say to the pupil 'X, I need you to stop tapping that pen' or 'X, I need you to put the pen down' or 'X, please put the pen down'. These requests tell the pupil what to do and there is no room for a pupil to say they did not understand the instruction. Always ensure a pupil has direct eye contact with you when you give your instruction. In the early days of meeting a class for the first time, it is highly likely you will forget pupils' names. A strong recommendation is to have a copy of your seating plan (there is an example in Appendix 2) on your desk at all times, so that pupils can be referred to by name. Managing your tone is also very important. Pupils must be able to recognise when you need their attention. Practice voice inflections and reap the rewards!

Additionally, within the computing classroom, you may have to ask all pupils to turn off their monitors when you address them, to ensure you have their full attention and that they are not distracted by anything on their monitors. Depending on the classroom layout you may also have to ask pupils to turn and face you. This point is further developed in Chapter 3 in the section 'The computing classroom'.

- **Delegation** – being able to identify tasks that others around you can do well is an important skill in this profession. If you can share out work it frees you up to then deliver your lesson without distraction and helps with time management. Delegation within the classroom and computing department occurs at many different levels. This can take the form of pupils, who hand out and collect in resources and it can be in terms of support staff who support one side of the room while you support the other side of the room during a main activity and then this is swapped over mid lesson. This will assist with behaviour management as the class is checked on for all the learning time. For example, a head of department may suggest, in the case of a particularly difficult topic, that each teacher in the department researches a part of that topic and then that this research is put together to produce a teaching resource, as opposed to each teacher attempting to re-invent the wheel themselves.

- **Management** – there are not many other jobs where on the first day of the job you must manage a large team of 20–30 (pupils) and in which the team will change at least five times during the day.

  You will be managing a large team with differing personalities and trying to get each team member to make satisfactory individual progress as well as meeting the overall lesson objectives; this is challenging and you must do it all within set time frames. Time management is essential. Thus, when planning and preparing for a lesson it is wise to be aware of how much time will be spent on a task and activity. This will assist greatly in classroom management. One big area within managing your personal workload is allowing sufficient time for marking pupils' work. Many new entrants into the profession underestimate the amount of time required to mark books or digital artefacts such as programs.

It is worth noting that the computer science teacher can also make use of automated assessment tools to support the marking process. There is more detail on such tools in Chapter 3.

TOP TIP

Employ a range of marking strategies, such as peer marking, self-assessment, focused marking against specific areas, and so on. You can put numbers against the area to be corrected and the pupil can then check what those numbers mean from a central sheet and write out the full correction statement or model answer.

At this point, if you haven't already, do self-assess against the grids in Appendix 1. Where there are attributes, knowledge and skills which need to be developed, it is advisable to speak to your mentor or line manager and ask to observe another teacher within or out of your department or year group who has developed those areas so that you can learn. If you have a strong area, share this with your colleagues at team meetings and others may observe you and learn. Teaching is a team effort!

All teachers will at some point in their career find that in addition to teaching a class of say 30 pupils, a teacher may have several adult assistants within the classroom. These assistants are usually there to support a learner or specific learners with needs; examples of such needs are dyslexia, dyscalculia, behaviour issues and social issues, such as anxiety, and so on. The teacher will also need to manage these additional staff. This is sometimes challenging for a new teacher as the focus tends to be on the pupils; however, all supporting staff must be clearly briefed on your expectations of them in the classroom. Table 2.3 suggests how some of the attributes, knowledge and skills discussed earlier are also transferable when managing additional staff in the classroom.

Table 2.3 Managing additional staff – Attributes, knowledge and skills

Attribute	Explanation in relation to managing additional staff
Organisation and preparation	All support staff need to have a copy of the Scheme of Work, lesson objectives and access to materials required
Reflection	At the end of a lesson or even during a lesson, communicate with additional staff and get feedback on the lesson or on individual pupils; this helps to give an all-round approach to inform future planning
Listening	Sometimes support staff are assigned to a particular pupil and see that pupil in a range of lessons across the school. Ask for information on that pupil's progress in other subjects and what works well. It is always good to have a broad view beyond the computing classroom

(Continued)

Table 2.3 (Continued)

Knowledge	Explanation of knowledge
Technical skills	Supporting staff do need to understand key terminology used within the subject and to be able to help pupils break down and explain problems. They should also be comfortable using software and hardware to an acceptable degree (this will be determined by your requirements)
Understanding of local and national initiatives for the subject and education in general	If supporting staff are attending subject or departmental meetings they will be getting a feel for this; however, if they are not it is a good idea to share these initiatives so that everyone understands what is happening in the subject – for example, support staff should be aware of enrichment activities for your subject and attend these activities to ensure that they are accessible to all pupils

General skills	Explanation of general skills
Leadership	Invite support staff along to departmental meetings so that they can contribute to the department and understand the departmental and school vision. This is key whether you are a teacher or a head of department
Ability to maintain good relationships with other staff	This skill should speak for itself in this section. As we have seen, the additional staff in the classroom provide a valuable role and link between the teacher and pupils. Having good rapport with supporting staff will reap benefits

Table 2.3 (Continued)

General skills	Explanation of general skills
Celebrate achievement	Always thank the staff at the end of each lesson for the work that they did and where possible identify stand out moments where they assisted a pupil in making progress
Delegate	Depending upon the type of support staff that you have, it may be possible to delegate jobs such as resource preparation, for example, loading files onto a virtual learning environment, sourcing news articles, and so on
Management	Always give additional staff clear instructions on what you require them to do and any changes to the Scheme of Work, lesson or seating plan

In addition to managing support staff, a teacher will also find that they need to manage parents and parental expectations. Always refer to a more senior colleague and school policies for support and guidance on this matter. Further real-life application of attributes, knowledge and skills can be found in the case study evidence in Chapter 5.

SPOTLIGHT ON JOB ADVERTS AND JOB TITLES

Having got a feel for what the role requires from you, it is time to turn our attention to the recruitment process. The purpose of this section is to help you in finding the right job when working your way through a myriad of adverts. A scan of the recruitment pages for secondary teaching roles in computer science will return lots of other similar titles such as:

- Teacher of Computer Science and Information Technology.
- Curriculum Leader of Computing.
- Computing Science Teacher KS 3–5.
- Assistant Head of Computing.
- Lead Practitioner of Computer Science.
- Computing Teacher.
- Teacher of ICT and Computer Science.
- Teacher of Computing and ICT.
- Lead Teacher of Computing.
- Secondary Computing Teacher.

This is just a snapshot of job titles noted in the recruitment pages; as you can see the terms, ICT, Computing and Computer Science are all being used and in some cases when we drill down into the advert, they are being used interchangeably. Think back to the explanations given in Chapter 1. It makes for interesting thought on what each of these adverts is seeking. Remember, the curriculum is still relatively new!

For primary colleagues, how is recruitment managed? Expectations from the job details would be within your classroom teacher role unless there is a dedicated computer science or computing teacher at your school. For example, an advert for a primary teacher may be advertised as 'Year 3 teacher vacancy' and a year 3 teacher would teach all subjects in the curriculum as opposed to being a subject specialist in one area, which is the case in secondary.

Most adverts tend to offer **overall detail on the school** which generally follows the lines of:

- school motto and vision;
- location;

- facilities across the school and within the computing department;
- staff benefits;
- reporting structure;
- OFSTED rating;[37]
- Progress 8 and Attainment 8 scores[38] (for secondary schools). For primary schools, key stage 2 performance[39] data are sometimes shown.

Then there are two other information documents that will be provided: a **job description** document and a **person specification** document.

The job description tends to describe the role that you will be doing and gives further detail on the computing department, such as the equipment within the department and how well they are resourced. There should also be mention of teaching and learning, assessment and reporting, classroom and behaviour management and the curriculum being followed.

TOP TIPS – LOOK FOR:

- Mention of the schools pass rates at GCSE and A-level/ performance data.
- Mention of the awarding body specification being followed.
- Programming languages being taught.
- Enrichment activities available for pupils.

These are additional elements to the job that are important to you in making a success of the role. If they are not mentioned it is worth finding out this information before the job interview or even asking some of these questions at interview.

The **person specification** of job adverts will cover the attributes, knowledge and skills to which we have previously referred. There will also be mention of essential versus desired qualifications for the role; this is where your degree, QTS and additional qualifications such as the BCS Certificate in Computer Science Teaching, BCS SKE Course in Computer Programming, Microsoft Office Specialist Certification and so on will be relevant.

TOP TIPS

Be aware of adverts that use woolly terms such as 'confident programmer' – this is where you need to know the programming language used and the previous experiences of the pupils, as this will be a determining factor in getting the most out of the pupils and in making a success of the role.

We will now analyse job advert excerpts from two secondary schools – Sunbury Manor School, Surrey and Bradley Stoke Community School, Bristol (the full adverts are in Appendix 3). Sunbury Manor is a mixed secondary academy with approximately 1,025 pupils on roll. Bradley Stoke Community School is also a mixed secondary academy with approximately 1,117 pupils.

Note that both advert excerpts are for the role of 'Teacher of Computing and IT'. These have been selected not only to allow a comparison between the same role in different schools, but also to show you two examples of a role which includes teaching computer science in a wider context. You will find many such roles when browsing job boards.

Example 1

Sunbury Manor School – Surrey. The position for a Teacher of Computing and IT was advertised (this role encompasses teaching computer science). The application pack contained the following items:

- welcome letter from the head teacher – shown in Figure 2.2;
- job description – Figure 2.3;
- person specification – Table 2.4;
- additional information – Figure 2.4;
- recruitment and selection policy (not included in this book due to size).

Figure 2.2 Sunbury Manor – Head teacher welcome letter

Sunbury Manor School began the new academic year with the best GCSE results the school has ever seen and we are now placed in the top 25% of similar schools nationally.

In March 2016, we had an Ofsted inspection and I am delighted to share some of the key highlights below. The full letter can be viewed on the school website www.sunburymanor.surrey.sch.uk and it confirms that the school continues to be good and that the good quality of education has been maintained since the last inspection. We were delighted that they stated that;

This is a very inclusive school that serves its community well.

The school is a safe, happy and harmonious environment.

You and other leaders have developed an aspirational culture where the main focus is on the quality of teaching and learning. Consequently, teaching remains good.

Behaviour around the school is good, with calm and orderly movement between classes and at break times. Pupils are respectful of their environment with very little litter or damage seen in the buildings. Pupils are polite and helpful to visitors, holding doors open for them. Pupils wear their uniform smartly and are proud of their school.

(Continued)

Figure 2.2 (Continued)

I am so proud of our students, staff and governors and so pleased that their hard work and dedication has been recognised. We are united as a school and face all challenges with determination and relentless positivity and were delighted by a recent parent comment that we are "a school that is concerned with the whole well-being of their children, rather than just being a results factory."

Here information is given on the school's results, highlights from the most recent OFSTED inspection and where to find further information on the school's OFSTED inspection. The head teacher also praises all involved in the success of the school. This gives the prospective applicant an idea of what is important to the school.

Selected from the job description are a few points which are not always immediately obvious to new entrants into the profession; these are highlighted in Figure 2.3. These include points such as setting homework regularly, differentiation, working with specialist staff to differentiate for groups such as SEN pupils, assessment, the ongoing need for safeguarding and keeping subject knowledge and wider teaching knowledge up to date.

Figure 2.3 Sunbury Manor – Computing and IT teacher job description

Teaching and Learning

Use a variety of methods and approaches (including differentiation) to match curricular objectives and the range of pupil needs, and ensure equal opportunity for all pupils.

Set homework regularly (in accordance with the School homework policy), to consolidate and extend learning and encourage pupils to take responsibility for their own learning.

(Continued)

Figure 2.3 (Continued)

Work with SEN staff and support staff (including prior discussion and joint planning) in order to benefit from their specialist knowledge and to maximise their effectiveness within lessons.

Monitoring, Assessment, Recording, Reporting, and Accountability

Be immediately responsible for the processes of identification, assessment, recording and reporting for the pupils in their charge.

Assess pupils' work systematically and use the results to inform future planning, teaching and curricular development.

Be familiar with statutory assessment and reporting procedures and prepare and present informative, helpful and accurate reports to parents.

Keep an accurate register of pupils for each lesson.

Subject Knowledge and Understanding

Keep up-to-date with research and developments in pedagogy and the subject area.

Professional Standards and Development

Maintain a working knowledge and understanding of teachers' professional duties as set out in the current School Teachers' Pay and Conditions document, and teachers' legal liabilities and responsibilities relating to all current legislation, including the role of the education service in safeguarding children.

Be aware of the role of the Governing Body of the School and support it in performing its duties.

Continuing Professional Development

Undertake any necessary professional development as identified in the School Improvement Plan taking full

(Continued)

Figure 2.3 (Continued)

> advantage of any relevant training and development available.
>
> Maintain a professional portfolio of evidence to support the Performance Management process – evaluating and improving own practice.

What now follows are some interview tips based upon an analysis of the Sunbury Manor School – Computing and IT teacher job description:

- **Teaching and learning** – discuss differentiation methods that you have used and the results achieved, discuss homework systems or schedules that you have used or followed and their effectiveness. Be prepared to discuss personalised and independent learning and the impact upon pupils, including any collaboration from SEN departments to ensure that each individual achieves.

- **Monitoring, assessment, recording, reporting and accountability** – be prepared to discuss involvement in report writing and giving feedback to parents and carers at parents' evenings. Let the interviewer know systems and methods that you have utilised to keep track of pupil progress, and how effective these systems were. Mention any marking strategies used and the impact upon your teaching and upon the pupils; remark on your reflective practise and how it has helped to influence subsequent lessons. Mention register systems used – either paper-based or electronic systems.

- **Subject knowledge and understanding** – discuss any pedagogical styles used and how they impacted upon the pupils – did the pedagogy affect the outcomes? Mention anything topical in the news around the curriculum.

- **Professional standards** – refer to any involvement with school governors. If you have not been involved with governors, Appendix 8 offers a reference with more information on school governors. Be aware of the Teachers Pay and Conditions Document – ask questions related to the school around this document, for example, ask what is done for the well-being of all staff, you will find many schools offer healthcare or gym memberships; this will show that you are conversant with the document.

- **Continuing Professional Development (CPD)** – mention all CPD that you have undertaken and its impact upon your practice. Perhaps even take along a folder of examples of work that you have produced and how they have been used in the classroom.

The person specification details the qualifications, knowledge and understanding, skills and personal attributes which a prospective applicant should possess. These are further broken down into Essential and Desirable qualities. A part of this specification is presented in Table 2.4. When going to interview, you need to be prepared to talk about each of these points and to provide examples of each one. Where possible, take along a portfolio of evidence to show to your prospective new employer.

Table 2.4 Sunbury Manor – Person specification

	Essential	Desirable
Qualifications and training	• Honours degree • Qualified teacher status	• Good honours degree in the subject you are teaching

(Continued)

Table 2.4 (Continued)

	Essential	Desirable
Experience	• Evidence of successful classroom teaching • Proven track record of teaching and motivating all ages and abilities • Ability to demonstrate high standards of classroom practice	• Involvement in working with students in extracurricular activities
Knowledge and understanding	• Awareness of child protection agenda • Able to devise and implement strategies for raising students' achievement in lessons • Committed to continued professional development • Knowledge of National Curriculum • Production of resources to aid effective learning	• Child protection training • Able to develop relevant use of ICT in lessons • Understanding of current issues in learning
Skills	• Ability to motivate and encourage students across the age and ability range	• Experience of some aspects of whole school initiatives

(Continued)

Table 2.4 (Continued)

	Essential	Desirable
	• Ability to work successfully as part of a team, sharing good practice • Ability to support and help manage change	• ICT skills

We will now analyse the Sunbury Manor School person specification in relation to preparing for an interview, as before:

- **Qualifications and training** – ensure that you have all certificates to prove that you have the qualification; some schools may ask to see these before interview and others upon a job offer.

- **Experience** – mention any involvement in running afterschool clubs and the impact upon pupils and the school community; mention any school trips that you have taken part in; if you have not been involved in any enrichment activity, offer ideas on what you feel you would be able to implement and give reasons as to why you feel this would be beneficial.

- **Knowledge and understanding** – as previously mentioned, take along a folder of evidence to support this, such as resources you have created, and be prepared to discuss their effectiveness – how would they be differentiated for differing groups? Mention risk assessments and safeguarding that you are aware of in relation to school trips and enrichment activities, such as ensuring there is someone first aid trained on a school trip or taking a register for afterschool activities, as while these are not in the formal classroom, a register still needs to be taken, as part of your duty of care to pupils.

- **Skills** – give specific examples of motivating pupils, such as through GCSE revision or targeted intervention sessions; be ready to talk about the impact on pupils and the school.

Many schools will provide additional detail in a job advert. In Figure 2.4 the applicant is given detail regarding the school's involvement with CAS, courses run and that there is an ongoing CPD programme. All good points to look for, as in addition to you giving to the school, it is essential to know how the school will support your journey.

Figure 2.4 Sunbury Manor – Job advert additional information for candidate

Sunbury Manor is a lead school in the Computing at Schools (CAS) Network of Excellence and we are also a CAS hub. Our Director of Computing & Digital Learning is a CAS Master Teacher. At Sunbury Manor, you will also benefit from on-going CPD sessions which are run as part of our CAS Sunbury hub meetings.

We are a well-resourced department who take a lead in delivering a high-quality computing curriculum and are looking for a forward-thinking teacher who is enthusiastic and willing to share in our passion and vision for an outstanding department.

We have been early adopters of the new curriculum and have recently featured in DfE and CAS publications regarding the new Computing programme of study.

At key stage 4 we offer GCSE Computing, GCSE ICT and OCR Cambridge Nationals ICT. Additionally, all key stage 3 students follow the new Computing curriculum.

Source: www.eteach.com (link now expired)

In this additional information for the candidate, the school places emphasis on computing as they are active in the computing teachers' subject association network (CAS). There is mention of a well-resourced department – take note of the resources available when you go on a tour of the school and if these are not pointed out ask what resources are available to support teaching and learning.

The school mentions being featured in publications so before the interview, conduct research and read up on how the school was featured; this helps you in having more points to discuss at interview. Also of note here is the mention of courses followed.

Example 2

Bradley Stoke Community School – Bristol. The position for a Teacher of Computing and IT was advertised (computer science included here in computing – note particularly the lesson planning task in Figure 2.5). The application pack contained the following items:

- teacher job description – Table 2.5;
- person specification – Table 2.6;
- planning task and teaching episode **(made available after initial application and short listing)** – Figure 2.5;
- additional information – Appendix 3.

The teacher job description and person specification are similar to those of Sunbury Manor. With this job description, different parts have been picked out to the previous school; when these documents are read together the full picture of the role emerges.

Within the Bradley Stoke job description, shown in Table 2.5, your attention is drawn to safeguarding and there is specific mention of responsibilities as a form tutor. Teaching and learning (the core of teaching) is described, encompassing matters of discipline and behaviour (note these were mentioned in the other advert through the head teacher's letter). Staff development and how you will be supported in your career are also mentioned along with some of the colleagues with whom you you would need to develop effective working relationships. Remember teaching is a people business!

Table 2.5 Bradley Stoke Community School – Computing and IT teacher job description

Role profile	Teacher
Job purpose	1. To empower students to become independent learners and develop personal responsibilities as a member of the community as described in the Bradley Stoke Community School ideal learner profile.
	2. To facilitate and encourage learning which enables students to achieve high standards.
	3. To be responsible for the welfare and guidance of students which may include responsibility for a tutor group.
Accountabilities (actions)	**Strategic direction**
	1. Ensure that the 4Rs (Reflective, Resilient, Resourceful and Responsible) are explicit in learning and teaching.
	Teaching and learning
	2. Use systems for the recording, monitoring and target setting of individual students' progress according to department strategies.
	3. Maintain discipline in accordance with school's behaviour policy and demonstrate good practices in the classes taught with regard to attendance, appearance, uniform, punctuality, behaviour and independent learning (homework).
	4. Ensure that independent learning is set, marked and monitored according to the school's policy.

(Continued)

Table 2.5 (Continued)

Role profile	Teacher

5. To mark, grade and give written/ verbal and diagnostic feedback as required.

6. Contribute to the personal development aspects of the welfare and guidance system including mentoring and tutoring.

7. Manage effective rewards and sanctions for students in line with school policy.

Staff development

8. Maintain effective communication across subject teams and with other staff (e.g. Technicians, Student Support team, Learning Support team, Business team, etc.).

9. Engage in the school's continuous professional development programme by participating in arrangements for further training and professional development.

10. Engage actively in the Appraisal process.

11. Developing community links, including local, national and international networks.

Pastoral support

As a tutor:

12. To promote a learning focused approach to all tutor activities.

(Continued)

Table 2.5 (Continued)

Role profile	Teacher	
	13. To develop learning focused relationships with all members of the tutor group.	
	14. To register students, accompany them to assemblies, encourage their attendance at lessons and their participation in other aspects of school life.	
	15. To monitor the progress of students.	
Support provided	**Line management**	**Wider support**
	A Curriculum or Subject Team Leader will have responsibility for induction and coaching to maximise self-confidence and effectiveness in post.	Teachers will participate in local authority best practice forums and the school's professional development programme.

We will now analyse the Bradley Stoke Community School Computing and IT teacher job description in relation to interview preparation:

- **Job purpose** – here there is emphasis on independent learners. At interview, be prepared to discuss ways of supporting pupils in being independent learners; perhaps mention strategies such as Flipped Learning. How effective was the strategy, do strategies differ depending upon the groups of pupils? Mention any involvement with a tutor group, the types of activities in which the group participated and the effectiveness. Be prepared to reflect and offer ways of improvement.

- **Accountabilities** – note the mention of the 4Rs – Reflective, Resilient, Resourceful and Responsible. These are core to the school so match what you are saying to these areas and provide examples from your past experiences; show how you will be an asset to the school. Before interview, have a look at the school's website and familiarise yourself with the school policies; there is mention of 'behaviour management strategies' in this advert so read the school's policy on behaviour before the interview, mention strategies that you have used and their effectiveness. There is also mention of a marking policy – ensure that this is also read before interview. Discuss marking strategies that you have used in your own practice and the impact upon pupils – did strategy differ between groups? Did strategy depend on the type of work you were marking such as paper-based work or digital artefacts?

- **Staff development** – be ready to discuss examples of interaction with colleagues across different teams. Be able to answer questions on how you got the 'buy in' of other colleagues and what about dealing with 'perceived difficult' colleagues? Mention any community links that you have had in previous roles or, if you haven't, mention ones that you would like to foster and explain why; remember to relate this and show the impact upon pupils and the school environment.

- **Pastoral support** – discuss ways of monitoring pupil progress, in class, from lesson to lesson and between groups. Mention any other teams with whom you have liaised with when monitoring pupil progress. Of course, remember to talk about safeguarding and interactions with 'heads of years' and other tutors – mention the effectiveness of these meetings in helping each pupil to achieve.

It is worth noting that both schools also mention the pay scale (although not in the extracts) and reporting structure. If not within the advert, this information will be available on the school's website, which will have the full job advert and all related documentation. If this information is not available, it should most definitely be requested. More detail regarding pay scales is given in Chapter 4.

The person specification here (Table 2.6), is also similar to Sunbury Manor, however, the knowledge, skills and ability are all together. Note the similarities with the subject knowledge requirements, team player skills and in motivating and inspiring pupils. Also, think back to the knowledge, attributes and skills section: can you see the points feeding through into the advert?

Table 2.6 Bradley Stoke Community School – Person specification

	Essential	Desirable
Qualifications	1. Graduate status and appropriate teaching qualifications	1. Accredited professional development
Experience	1. Evidence of successful teaching which has had a demonstrable impact on student progress	1. Experience of working in a secondary school
	2. Experience of a range of strategies, approaches and resources for developing teaching and learning to meet a wide range of student abilities and needs	2. Training/ expertise in behaviour and/or learning support
	3. Evidence of continuing professional development	3. Experience of teaching and learning programmes beyond subject boundaries

(Continued)

Table 2.6 (Continued)

	Essential	Desirable
Knowledge, skills and abilities	1. Ability to teach computing and IT to key stage 3 and 4 2. Ability to motivate and inspire students 3. Excellent classroom teacher and interested in developing subject pedagogy 4. Excellent organisational skills 5. Excellent oral and written communication skills 6. Ideas about how to develop personalised learning and how to create independent learners 7. Evidence of collaborative approaches to work (team player) but also able to work independently 8. Sense of humour, flexibility and ability to remain positive at all times	An ability to teach programming **or** multimedia software skills and concepts up to key stage 5 to teach business to key stage 4 and 5 Able and keen to teach more than one subject An understanding of subject self-evaluation

(Continued)

Table 2.6 (Continued)

Essential	Desirable
9. Commitment to helping develop, lead and deliver enrichment experiences for all students, including educational visits	An ability to teach programming **or** multimedia software skills and concepts up to key stage 5
10. Commitment to working with local primary and secondary schools and community organisations	to teach business to key stage 4 and 5
	Able and keen to teach more than one subject
11. Commitment to developing links and networks locally, nationally and internationally	An understanding of subject self-evaluation

Further examination of this person specification shows in the knowledge section that there is mention of programming languages – mention the languages with which you are conversant and your depth of experience in the interview, ask which languages are in use at the school and what influenced that decision. There is the option to teach a second subject; this could be a form of career development for the right candidate; ask what the subject is and ascertain if you have the necessary subject knowledge; remember that this is a desirable and not essential factor. Discuss collaborative approaches to developing departmental resources, such as resources for teaching number systems, and how you have independently developed resources which you shared as best practice.

Be prepared to talk about a 'challenging day' and how you managed the situation and were able to bounce back (remember the key here is resilience). Additionally, mention any involvement with feeder schools. If you have not previously interacted with feeder schools, offer suggestions on links you would like to foster and explain how these would be beneficial to the school.

Another useful exercise at this point is seeing if you can identify where involvement in organisations such as CAS would play a role in this job description. For the desirable parts of the specification, it would also be good to have some idea of how you would plan to develop those areas if they are not currently a part of what you can offer the school. Let the interviewer know this information; have a frank discussion on how they can support you.

Bradley Stoke provides additional information which details the equipment with which the department is resourced (see Appendix 3) and a breakdown of the topics studied at each of the key stages. This is particularly useful at key stage 3, as schools are free to design their own curriculums. At key stage 4, knowing the awarding body and courses followed is important as this will help you to match your experience to what the school currently has in place.

Getting that teaching job!

Now that we have had an overview of the parts of a job advert, it is worth looking at some of the factors you should consider if you are applying for a first teaching job or changing between schools as an experienced teacher.

Covering letters

This is an opportunity to give the prospective employer a few highlights about your experiences.

TOP TIPS

Applicant

- Include postal address and other contact details such as email address and telephone number.

Addressee

- Always write to a named person, remember to use the correct title and spell names correctly.

- Include the school address at the top of the page.

Language and format

- Use short simple sentences.

- Avoid over using 'I', especially 'I' at the start of each paragraph.

- Use business or professional language.

- Use an appropriate font style.

Structure

- Attention-grabbing introduction.

- The key message.

- A strong conclusion.

- Keep the letter short – Maximum one page of A4.

Application forms

A correctly filled in application form is vital. It is surprising how many applicants do not get to interview stage due to not reading the instructions on a form.

Lesson planning

As part of the interview process you will be required to teach a sample lesson. This is usually from a set of pre-set topics by the interviewer. This is your opportunity to show subject knowledge, classroom management skills, lesson planning skills for an engaging lesson, resource planning, interpersonal skills and the ability to think on your feet in case an activity does not go to plan.

TOP TIPS

- If planning a computer-based lesson always have an unplugged activity as a backup.

- If teaching an unplugged lesson have at least one other way of demonstrating the same topic.

- Read the instructions carefully.

- Follow all instructions.

- Fill in all mandatory sections.

- Use the correct colour ink, as indicated on the application form, such as black ink.

- Focus on spelling, punctuation and grammar (SPaG).

The example at Figure 2.5 from Bradley Stoke Community School gives you an idea of a lesson planning task.

Figure 2.5 Bradley Stoke – Lesson planning task

PLANNING TASK

Computing and IT is a subject that requires students to develop good problem solving skills. Some students have a natural ability to think logically and develop their programming craft with relative ease.

However, there are students who enjoy the subject but struggle to understand and apply the core computational thinking concepts that underpin computer programming.

You will be asked to lead a 15-minute discussion with members of the Computing and IT team on how we might approach delivery of the programming component of the

(Continued)

Figure 2.5 (Continued)

GCSE Computer Science curriculum with those students in mind.

TEACHING EPISODE

Select one of the three objectives outlined below and plan, resource and deliver a 20-minute teaching episode based on it:

- Represent denary numbers in binary.
- Explain how the intellectual property of a digital asset is protected.
- Describe the hardware required to make a functioning computer system.

To aid with your planning, two class profiles detailing SEN, pupil premium (PP) and More Able Gifted and Talented (MAGT) needs have been provided for the two possible year 7 classes involved in the interview process. The room is equipped with a projector and 32 computers, spread across six rows. A layout of the classroom is provided.

Think of the top tip given earlier – on unplugged activities. How would you apply it here? Based upon your class profile (see Appendix 4), how might you wish to seat pupils based upon their needs (see seating plan in Appendix 2)? What if the pupils are already seated when you need to teach them? How would you approach this? Lots of food for thought.

Interview

This is your opportunity to talk about what you can offer the school both within the curriculum and beyond. At this point reflect on points 10 and 11 of the Bradley Stoke Community School person specification (Table 2.6).

The interview is also an opportunity to drill down and ask probing questions, such as which systems are in place to monitor underachievement, how are high achievers supported, how the school encourages uptake of the subject at GCSE and A-level for pupils in key groups such as girls, SEN, ethnicity, and so on, what are the key points of the school's development plan in relation to computing?

You can further talk about new ways of engaging pupils, such as ideas you have seen at trade shows or have had the benefit of observing while training. This is your moment to shine.

TOP TIPS

1. Be aware of current news stories around education and computing.

2. Research the school fully, have a look at the school's website and their key documents, find out about onsite parking, proximity to public transport, the possibility of receiving a free school lunch, incentives such as childcare vouchers, staff recognition schemes and so on.

3. Practise the interview beforehand.

4. Try to interview for as long as possible but do not over talk (there is a fine balance here).

5. Take breaths when talking – don't talk too quickly.

6. Ask for a question to be repeated if you do not understand or need to buy time to think of your answer.

7. Dress appropriately for the interview, such as business wear.

8. Arrive on time.

9. Remember body language is key – remain engaged with the interviewer, do not bite your nails, look down, out of the window, up at the ceiling or fidget.

THE ROLE OF THE COMPUTER SCIENCE TEACHER

10. Be aware of humour and do not make inappropriate jokes.
11. Ask when you should expect to hear an outcome.
12. Thank the interviewer.

The computer science teacher (and computing teacher) is a rare commodity; you need to ensure that you find the best school for your personality and the school that will support you in your career. Chapter 4 offers some ideas on where to look for teaching jobs.

3 STANDARDS, TOOLS, METHODS AND TECHNIQUES

In addition to the attributes, knowledge and skills covered in the previous chapter, success as a computer science teacher also depends on good knowledge of the standards, tools, methods and techniques that apply to the role. In this chapter, you will gain an understanding of standards for the teaching profession and examine pedagogy and assessment tools. There's also analysis of an example lesson plan, along with supporting resources and dialogue. There is focus on managing the computer science learning environment along with general classroom tips. An analysis of timetables is also covered, along with discussion on interactions with non-computer science colleagues. Additionally, there is identification of ways to promote computer science within schools and a section on diversity and inclusion in the classroom.

STANDARDS

This section covers standards from higher levels (government) through to lesson observations, OFSTED inspections, Attainment 8 and Progress 8 measures, SATs measures and school policies, which, when understood, lead to excellent understanding of the teaching profession and outstanding practice.

Skills Framework for the Information Age – SFIA

The first standard which we will investigate is the Skills Framework for the Information Age (SFIA). Governments use SFIA within education and training to ensure that the most suitable courses and certifications are chosen for the population. In a day-to-day teaching role, the words SFIA do not feature in the classroom, however the framework is most definitely in use. This standard is included here for an understanding of the wider picture of standards. Figure 3.1 gives an explanation from the SFIA website. You will be guided through from the top level of the framework down to the relevant section on teaching.

Figure 3.1 SFIA overview

1. 'The Skills Framework for the Information Age' (SFIA) is the global skills and competency framework that describes IT roles and the skills needed for them. It is supported by industry, backed by the UK government and adopted in organisations worldwide. SFIA is used in two ways, the first being to 'provide generic levels of responsibility, with descriptions at each of the seven levels for the following attributes: Autonomy · Influence · Complexity · Business Skills

2. To reflect experience and competency levels within SFIA. The definitions describe the behaviours, values, knowledge and characteristics that an individual should have in order to be identified as competent at that level. Each level has a guiding word or phrase that acts as a brief indicator: Follow · Assist · Apply · Enable · Ensure, Advise · Initiate, Influence · Set Strategy, Inspire, Mobilise'

Sources: www.bcs.org/upload/pdf/sfiaplus-flyer.pdf https://www.sfia-online. org/en/reference-guide https://www.sfia-online.org/en/how-sfia-works/ responsibilities-and-skills

The seven levels of the SFIA framework are shown in Figure 3.2 along with the related grading of importance.

Figure 3.2 The SFIA framework levels

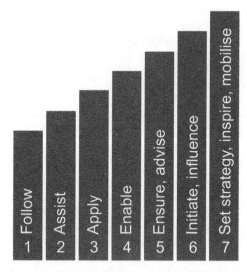

Source: https://www.sfia-online.org/en/how-sfia-works/responsibilities-and-skills

The subsection of the framework in Figure 3.3 shows the parts of the framework that relate to teaching: 5 – Ensure, advise and 6 – Initiate, influence. Hopefully you are connecting with these words from Chapter 2 when we looked at the attributes, knowledge and skills needed by a good computer science teacher, and starting to extend your understanding.

Figure 3.3 Skills and quality[40]

Category	Skill	Code	Level						
			1	2	3	4	5	6	7
Skills management	Teaching and subject formation	TEAC					░	░	

SFIA level 5

As we drill down further into SFIA level 5 – **Ensure and Advise** – the skills described by SFIA are shown in Figure 3.4.

Figure 3.4 SFIA level 5 explained

Autonomy

Works under broad direction and work is often self-initiated. Is fully responsible for meeting allocated technical and/or project / supervisory objectives. Establishes milestones and has a significant role in the assignment of tasks and/or responsibilities.

Influence

Influences the organisation, customers, suppliers, partners and peers on the contribution of own specialism. Build appropriate and effective business relationships. Make decisions which impact the success of assigned work, i.e. results, deadlines and budget and have significant influence over the allocation and management of resources appropriate to given assignments.

Complexity

Performs an extensive range and variety of complex technical and/or professional work activities. Undertake work which requires the application of fundamental principles in a wide and often unpredictable range of contexts. Understand the relationship between own specialism and wider customer / organisational requirements.

Business skills

Advises on the available standards, methods, tools and applications relevant to own specialism and can make

(Continued)

Figure 3.4 (Continued)

appropriate choices from alternatives. Analyse, design, plan, execute and evaluate work to time, cost and quality targets. Assess and evaluate risk. Communicate effectively, both formally and informally. Demonstrate leadership. Facilitate collaboration between stakeholders who have diverse objectives. Take all requirements into account when making proposals. Take initiative to keep skills up to date. Mentor colleagues. Maintain an awareness of developments in the industry. Analyse requirements and advise on scope and options for continuous operational improvement. Demonstrate creativity, innovation and ethical thinking in applying solutions for the benefit of the customer / stakeholder.

Source: www.bcs.org/content/ConWebDoc/32261

So how are these skills relevant to teachers? Level 5 is further explained in relation to the teaching and subject formation (TEAC) skill in SFIA as:

Delivers computing and IT curricula either in a formal educational context from primary through to tertiary level or in the workplace. Specialises in delivering Computing and IT education at the relevant educational level. Is aware of the techniques and methods used to evaluate and critique research in computing and IT education and applies good practice in learning content design, development and delivery.[41]

SFIA level 6

Drilling down further into SFIA level 6 – **Initiate and Influence** – the skills described by SFIA are shown in Figure 3.5.

Figure 3.5 SFIA level 6 explained

Autonomy

Has defined authority and accountability for actions and decisions within a significant area of work, including technical, financial and quality aspects. Establishes organisational objectives and assigns responsibilities.

Influence

Influences policy and strategy formation. Initiates influential relationships with internal and external customers, suppliers and partners at senior management level, including industry leaders. Makes decisions which impact the work of employing organisations, achievement of organisational objectives and financial performance.

Complexity

Has a broad business understanding and deep understanding of own specialism(s). Performs highly complex work activities covering technical, financial and quality aspects. Contributes to the implementation of policy and strategy. Creatively applies a wide range of technical and/or management principles.

Business skills

Absorbs complex information and communicates effectively at all levels to both technical and non-technical audiences. Manages and mitigates risk. Understands the implications of new technologies. Demonstrates clearleadership. Understands and communicates industry developments, and the role and impact of technology in the employing organisation. Promotes compliance with relevant legislation. Takes the initiative to keep both own and colleagues' skills up to date.

Source: www.bcs.org/content/ConWebDoc/32261

Again, we will now look at how these skills are relevant to teachers. Level 6 can be further explained in relation to the teaching and subject formation (TEAC) skill in SFIA as:

> Leads specification, development and delivery of computing and IT curricula in either a formal educational context, from primary through to tertiary level or in the workplace. Specialises in the advanced aspects of delivering Computing and IT education at the relevant educational level. Uses current techniques and methods to evaluate and critique research in computing and IT education and leads the development of good practice in learning content design, development and delivery.[42]

Hopefully this section has shown where teaching fits into the skills framework for the age in which we live. A useful exercise is to reflect on the SFIA explanations at level 5 and 6 and look at how much is done in your day-to-day job. There is or will be a perfect fit, whether you are starting out in the teaching profession or are an established teacher.

BCS Certificate in Computer Science Teaching

The BCS Certificate in Computer Science Teaching is a standard which shows that you have the required knowledge to perform your role. This is a Continuing Professional Development (CPD) form of accreditation which can be undertaken by teachers while on the job or as part of a training degree. The certificate is evidence based around experiential learning and fits with the environment in which the teacher works. Examples of this are attendance at CAS Hub meetings and reflecting on skills and knowledge gained, or attending CAS regional or national conferences or other teaching conferences. The programming project is of your choice and needs to reflect the programming knowledge and skills that you require for teaching. (Case study 1 in Chapter 5 includes mention of undertaking this qualification.) The classroom investigation looks at computer science pedagogy such as paired programming and this is evaluated. Figure 3.6 shows the parts of the qualification.

Figure 3.6 Structure of the BCS Certificate in Computer Science Teaching

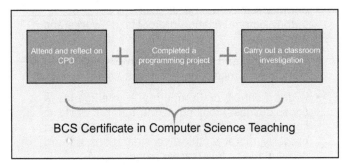

Source: www.computingatschool.org.uk/certificate

Subject knowledge requirements

As previously mentioned in the 'Attributes, knowledge and skills' section in the previous chapter, the DfE has published a guide to the knowledge required to teach computer science at both primary and secondary level. A look at the overview to this guide, as shown in Figure 3.7, discusses the key concepts.

Figure 3.7 Key concepts of computer science

Demonstrate understanding of the key concepts associated with the following areas:

- Language, Machines & Computation – languages, algorithms, machines and computational models
- Data and representation – data representation, data storage, data transmission, data structures, digital and analogue conversion

(Continued)

Figure 3.7 (Continued)

- Communication & Co-ordination – input-process-output, communication protocols, networks and the internet
- Abstraction and Design – hardware, software, simulation & modelling, interfaces, categorisation
- Wider Context of Computing – intelligence & consciousness, looking at the natural world in computational terms, creativity & intellectual property, moral & ethical considerations, uses of computing and jobs/career paths

(These are Expert group's recommendations)

Sources: www.education.gov.uk
http://media.education.gov.uk/assets/files/pdf/s/subject%20knowledge%20
requirements%20for%20entry%20into%20cs%20teacher%20training.pdf

When commencing on the journey of teaching this specialist subject, one needs to be sure of these key concepts and have clear examples in mind.

Teacher standards

So far, we have looked at industry standards, possible qualification standards and concepts of the subject; however, underpinning all of this is what it takes to teach. Consequently, the teachers' standards are relevant at this point. The teachers' standards come into force as a trainee and when a teacher has achieved qualified teacher status (QTS). The teaching standards are used to assess the performance of teachers. The standards have two parts: Part one – Teaching, and Part two – Personal and Professional Conduct. Figure 3.8 shows the Part one overview statements.

There are sub points to each of the points above and it is recommended to read the references and be conversant with the sub points.

Figure 3.8 Overview of teachers' standards – Part one

- Set high expectations which inspire, motivate and challenge pupils.
- Promote good progress and outcomes by pupils.
- Demonstrate good subject and curriculum knowledge.
- Plan and teach well-structured lessons.
- Adapt teaching to respond to the strengths and needs of all pupils.
- Make accurate and productive use of assessment.
- Manage behaviour effectively to ensure a good and safe learning environment.
- Fulfil wider professional responsibilities.

Sources: https://www.gov.uk/government/uploads/system/uploads/attachment_data/file/301107/Teachers__Standards.pdf
https://www.gov.uk/government/uploads/system/uploads/attachment_data/file/283566/Teachers_standard_information.pdf

Part two (Figure 3.9) details how a teacher is expected to behave on the job and contains statements which define the behaviour and attributes required by the standard.

Figure 3.9 Teachers' standards – Part two

Teachers uphold public trust in the profession and maintain high standards of ethics and behaviour, within and outside school, by:

- treating pupils with dignity, building relationships rooted in mutual respect, and at all times observing proper boundaries appropriate to a teacher's professional position

(Continued)

Figure 3.9 (Continued)

- having regard for the need to safeguard pupils' well-being, in accordance with statutory provisions showing tolerance of and respect for the rights of others

- not undermining fundamental British values, including democracy, the rule of law, individual liberty and mutual respect, and tolerance of those with different faiths and beliefs

- ensuring that personal beliefs are not expressed in ways which exploit pupils' vulnerability or might lead them to break the law.

Teachers must have proper and professional regard for the ethos, policies and practices of the school in which they teach, and maintain high standards in their own attendance and punctuality.

Teachers must have an understanding of, and always act within, the statutory frameworks which set out their professional duties and responsibilities.

Source: https://www.gov.uk/government/uploads/system/uploads/attachment_data/file/283566/Teachers_standard_information.pdf

By now you should be able to see how these standards fit together and how they link with the attributes, knowledge and skills from Chapter 2.

Lesson observations

Once you are employed as a teacher, schools observe teachers at regular intervals throughout the year, depending upon the experience and needs of the teacher. These are formal lesson observations, the purpose of which is to ensure that the quality of teaching and learning across the school is consistently meeting the needs of learners. A lesson observation should not be seen as additional work, and there should certainly be no need to be worried. Just teach to your usual outstanding standard and all will be fine. Lesson observations are usually carried out by a senior member of staff such as a head of department or a member of the Senior Leadership Team (SLT).[43] There is some guidance on lesson observation protocol available on the National Union of Teachers (NUT) website.[44]

Usually you will be notified of when the lesson observation will take place and after the observation you should receive written feedback, in a timely manner. The feedback should summarise the focus of the observation and highlight outstanding practice and any areas for development. If a follow up observation is required, detail needs to be provided for the reasons why.

Currently, lessons are not graded, as they were in the past. The focus of the observation should be developmental, to ensure that you develop your practise. It is advisable to check within your school for their lesson observation protocol.

School policies

All schools have internal policies. These serve as standards which explain a particular school's stance on certain matters and the course of action to be taken on issues arising from those matters. There are also statutory policies for schools and guidance on policies available from the DfE. Examples of some of the policies that can be found in schools are detailed below. This list is not meant to be exhaustive and when in school it is your duty to familiarise yourself with all policies and procedures:

1. anti-bullying;
2. equal opportunities;
3. use of social media;
4. supporting pupils with medical conditions;
5. rewards and sanctions;

6. safeguarding or child protection;
7. health and safety;
8. data protection policy;
9. special education needs;
10. recruitment and selection policy (note that this was included in the Sunbury Manor job application pack seen in Chapter 2).

OFSTED

Now that we are aware of what schools are doing to ensure standards are met internally, you may be wondering who ensures that all schools are performing in a consistent manner.

This job is carried out by OFSTED.

Ofsted is the Office for Standards in Education, Children's Services and Skills. OFSTED inspect and regulate services that care for children and young people, and services providing education and skills for learners of all ages.

Source: https://www.gov.uk/government/organisations/ofsted

Schools are inspected at intervals by a team of OFSTED inspectors. The notice time given to schools for an inspection can change from year to year. See https://www.gov.uk/government/organisations/ofsted/about to keep abreast of the latest OFSTED inspection guidance.

Many teachers can get anxious about an OFSTED inspection, however, as a rule of thumb, as long as your teaching has always been at a high standard, pupils are well behaved, school policies are followed, there is evidence of progress by pupils, safeguarding, diversity and an inclusive classroom are evident, there really is nothing to fear.

OFSTED inspectors will spend a brief amount of time in your classroom before moving onto another classroom as part of their inspection. At the end of the inspection period, the head teacher and SLT receive the OFSTED report. Schools are currently graded: Outstanding (1), Good (2), Requires Improvement (3) or Inadequate (4). The inspection report will highlight the school's outstanding and good features. Should next steps be required these will also be listed and the school will receive a grading. During your teaching career, you will hear about schools that have received inadequate OFSTED ratings; the report for such schools will be very detailed regarding their next steps. Visit https://www.gov.uk/find-ofsted-inspection-report or https://reports.ofsted.gov.uk/ to find inspection reports for schools.

Progress 8 and Attainment 8

This is a new measure introduced in 2016 for secondary schools. The reasoning behind this standard is to ensure that each school offers a broad and balanced curriculum at key stage 4. Remember in Chapter 1, when progress from primary through to secondary school was mentioned, this becomes relevant when a Progress 8 score is worked out at key stage 4. Figure 3.10 summarises this standard. For a deeper understanding of this standard and where computer science fits, further reading is recommended.[45]

Figure 3.10 Progress 8 and Attainment 8 summary

Progress 8 aims to capture the progress a pupil makes from the end of primary school to the end of secondary school. It is a type of value added measure, which means that pupils' results are compared to the actual achievements of other pupils with the same prior attainment.

Attainment 8 measures the achievement of a pupil across 8 qualifications including mathematics (double weighted) and English (double weighted), 3 further qualifications that count in the English Baccalaureate (Ebacc) measure and 3 further qualifications that can be GCSE qualifications.

Source: https://www.gov.uk/government/uploads/system/uploads/attachment_data/file/583857/Progress_8_school_performance_measure_Jan_17.pdf

The equivalent of Progress and Attainment 8 measures at primary level is the 'Primary key stage 2 performance in Reading, Writing and Maths'.[46]

TOOLS

To enhance the learning experience, a teacher can make use of several pedagogical and assessment tools. Some of these are discussed below.

Virtual Learning Environments (VLE), of which examples include *FROG, Fronter* and *Moodle*. A VLE allows you to put a variety of media (text, images, podcasts, animations, videos) online to support both in and out of class learning. The media can also be hyperlinked to external sources. Documents such as the Scheme of Work and specifications should also be available on the VLE. Most learning environments can be accessed on a variety of platforms (PC, laptop, tablet computers, other mobile devices such as smartphones) and therefore can reach a wide audience in most school populations, whether during teaching time or outside class; for example, for homework, catch-up or re-enforcement of knowledge.

Pupils can view the material online or download and reference or complete and then upload it back to the VLE. This enables tracking of complete or incomplete work by the teacher and parents, thus allowing for a level of parental engagement. By tracking online, a record of activity is generated, which in turn saves you work and time in tracking your pupils. VLEs also allow for collaboration and working on a single document, which is a skill that pupils will need in the workplace.

Another feature of VLEs is built-in lesson planning tools. Many also provide Assessment for Learning (AfL)[47] features such as self-assessment quizzes. Additionally, they contain built-in emailing or messaging systems and some have forum functionality, both of which again are ways of promoting sharing, good online behaviour and respect of each other's opinions in a safe environment.

The VLE is powerful as long as the school infrastructure is good, to allow for a fast VLE service. There are a few downsides of a VLE. Firstly a teacher does have to put in time to learn to use the VLE effectively as they contain many features; however, some schools do have technicians who manage quite a bit of the VLE. Another downside is that in the case of power failure (this is rare), then there would be no access to teaching and learning materials. These two downsides are small points, but the biggest one is that all teachers should be cautious in ensuring that the VLE does not become a dumping ground for resources. Time does need to be set aside to 'audit or clean-up' the VLE on occasion to ensure that it serves the needs of the learners and the department effectively.

School-led and crowd-sourced platforms, such as **'Project Quantum',** cover key stages 1–5. Quantum contains thousands of questions with a focus on CT, making use of formative assessment and providing essential AfL data. Teachers can use the questions in the system or upload their own (these are quality checked); this makes for a free online national database of questions that are also automatically marked. Essentially, Quantum looks at a solution for all teachers, as opposed to just an individual classroom solution. At the time of writing this project has just been launched, so expect to hear more.

Game-based learning platforms, of which *Kahoot* is an example. Kahoot can also be used for quizzes, discussion and surveys. Here we will focus on quizzes. The teacher creates the multiple choice or single answer quiz questions they wish to ask the pupils. Once a question is created, images, videos and diagrams can be added to the question to support pupils, thus making the activity appealing to all types of learners. Pupils answer the questions in real time which allows for a fun element and high engagement. The main question is displayed on the board and pupils can answer or select the correct answer on their own devices or via devices provided to them (remember to check the school policy on use of personal mobiles in the classroom). The teacher can also see which questions were answered correctly or incorrectly and use this to inform future planning. There is also functionality to monitor progress by playing in 'ghost mode' against previous scores or to beat the high score. Kahoot allows for a social and collaborative learning experience in the computing classroom. Remember SMSC!

Cloud-based pupil response tools, of which *Socrative* is an example. With this tool you, as the teacher, have a few options, such as creating a quiz for your own teaching or downloading a quiz created by another teacher in your department. When used in class, Socrative gives instant feedback on questions answered correctly or incorrectly. It can be set up to display this on the pupil's monitor or only on the teacher's monitor. Data on quiz results can be downloaded into spreadsheet format and analysed, thus producing much needed assessment data on pupils who have grasped the necessary knowledge versus those who are struggling and thus helps to inform planning. Socrative contains a quick question option, which can be used as a formative assessment tool. This option is provided as multiple choice, true or false or short answer questions. Socrative also provides a 'space race' feature where pupils can compete against other groups of pupils as set by the teacher. The 'Exit ticket' is used similarly to a plenary to check understanding before the end of the lesson.

Online learning community tools, such as *Memrise*, which started off as a tool to teach languages; however, as the community grew, other courses were added. Computing features in the 'professional and careers courses' section. There is a wealth of learning resources here for a variety of programming languages and computer theory. Memrise serves as an additional tool to enhance the learning process, for example by being a revision aid. There are categories on Memrise and within those categories you can learn words and meanings; for example, in the 'Introduction to Python' section, there are basic words to learn such as 'Editor'. A definition is presented and you can choose to have 'help' to remember that definition through either a pre-created 'mem' (short for memory) or you can make your own mem. Building the mem is done in guided steps: association, imagination (image) and visualisation, and this helps to increase retention of information and learning. Memrise supports multimedia and there are multiple choice quizzes, fill in the answer questions and a variety of learning methods used around topics, against which you can self-assess.

Interactive White Boards (IWB), examples of which are ***Promethean*** and ***Smart Board***. These also allow for a level of interactivity within the classroom and appeal to pupils with different learning styles such as kinaesthetic, auditory and visual. Pupils can touch the board and manipulate elements on the board using their fingers, mouse or touch pens. They can click, copy, drag and select using the board. Videos or presentations can be displayed on the IWB allowing pupils to listen or view or both. Using the 'IWB pens' the board can be written on, and the writing captured and embedded into presentations which can then be stored on the VLE as a resource for the class. The IWB allows for collaborative learning and can be highly effective in small group work activities or small classes.

The IWB is excellent for demonstrations; as the teacher you can demonstrate how software works to the whole class at the same time. IWBs also have additional features such as a screen shade tool, so that you can hide or show parts of the main screen, thus focusing the attention of your learners during teaching and demonstrations. Some examples of additional tools are the spotlight tool, which again is used for drawing attention to a part of the screen, the magnifier for gaining a detailed view and the calculator for carrying out mathematical elements.

If you are particularly brave in the classroom, you may wish to try out making a 'scribe video'[48] when using the IWB. This can then be saved to the VLE as a learning resource.

Content-sharing tools, an example of which is *Padlet*. Think of Padlet as giving out post-it notes and pupils writing comments or drawing images and then putting them on a wall or board. Padlet is the digital version of a post-it note. Pupils use their online 'post it' to make comments and they can also add media to the post.

Benefits of this virtual 'post it' wall are that the wall can be customised, saved and referenced later on. Padlet walls can be embedded into blogs or into the VLE. Additionally, pupils can see each other's 'post-its' in real time. The wall can also be password protected (which you should do as part of safeguarding) and pupils can have online safety re-enforced through this activity. As the teacher, you can also moderate posts before they are posted onto the wall. To encourage whole class participation, posts can be made anonymously; alternatively pupil names can be displayed. Padlet is a great tool for collaboration and discussion, which lends itself to being respectful of the opinions of others. Remember SMSC and British Values at this point!

Massive Open Online Courses (MOOCs), an example of which is *Codecademy*. The use of a MOOC for flipped learning or to extend learning is great. It can be used as a self-learning or supporting tool or for embedding knowledge. For example, Codecademy supports pupils in learning coding concepts, which can be further explored in the classroom. The pedagogy in use on Codecademy is through scaffolding and progress, interactive activities and quizzes. Additionally, some awarding bodies, such as OCR,[49] have a MOOC which has the specification broken down into its parts with supporting text, video and images. Multiple choice tests are provided as a way of self-assessing knowledge and worksheets are provided for written answers. MOOCs allow for tracking of progress, which in turn provides valuable data and information for you as the teacher.

Classroom management software – examples include *Netsupport* and *Impero*. As the name implies, this is software used in the classroom to manage the computers and thus pupils in the room using these computers. This type of software allows the teacher to take control of all the computers in the room and display what is on the teacher's computer and IWB onto all of the monitors in the room, thus ensuring that all pupils are viewing the same thing at the same time, which is highly effective during demonstrations. Teachers can also interact remotely with the PC of an individual pupil if required. The software can be used to restrict access to certain websites, to keep the class focused. There is also the ability to lock and restrict specific computers. Some classroom management tools also have in-built AfL features.

Homework management tools – such as *Show my Homework*. The teacher assigns homework to classes online. Pupils and parents are emailed what homework needs to be done and due dates. Completed homework can then be submitted and marked online. Tools such as this also include quizzes and tests which are auto marked, which provides the teacher with valuable data and the ability to identify gaps in learning. You may have noticed that this tool relies on computers and online availability. However, you may find yourself in a school with pupils from lower socio-economic groupings who do not readily have access to online services. One way of making homework accessible to them is through 'Homework Booklets', which contain all the information that they need and space to write answers. Of course, this method is not self-marking, but it is inclusive. In Case Study 1 in Chapter 5, there is reference to the use of homework booklets to allow for participation from all pupils.

Having looked at a variety of tools for supporting the pupil, it is wise at this point to mention CPD tools being used by schools when looking at teaching as the profession. Many schools are adopting online CPD tools; an example of this is Blue Sky Education. For example, within the 'Blue Sky' environment, teachers keep track of CPD events attended and the impact upon their practice. Observation reports, responses to observations and self-evaluations are also stored in this online platform. Teachers can also collate evidence for progression up the pay scales. Additionally, Blue Sky has functionalities such as a messaging system and a 'social environment' for connecting to teachers in other schools. Of course, in computer science, a lot of subject knowledge CPD is already taking place either through CAS Hubs or online courses, such as Future Learn.[50]

METHODS

So, you are standing in front of a class. What method(s) will you employ to ensure that pupils engage with the knowledge and skills which they will gain in your room? How will they remember your lesson? A quote from a teacher is needed at this point!

'Think of your lesson in the language of the pupils – is your lesson RINGing* or MINGing?'

Steve Clarke
Director of Computing and Curriculum Consultant
* RINGing – Relevant, Interesting, Naughty or a Giggle.

At this point let's think of the lesson plan and resources which will be used within the lesson. We will now examine a key stage 3 lesson on Logic Gates and Truth Tables as an example.

Figure 3.11 shows that upon entering the classroom the lesson topic is clearly stated. Pupils have a task on arrival, they are asked to recall and link the keywords to prior knowledge; in this case pupils had previous lessons on 'Boolean operators' and 'Searching the internet'. The starter is also time bonded. Having a starter on arrival ensures that the lesson starts right away, behaviour issues are eliminated and allows you (albeit for a limited time) to conduct activities such as taking the register or dealing with a pupil who does not have the correct equipment or any other matter that may arise.

Figure 3.11 Starter activity or task on arrival

Title: Logic Gates and Truth Tables

Starter:

- What is the link between the following words? Where have you come across these words before in computing?

AND	**OR**	**NOT**

Write your answer in your book and then login

Time: 1 minute

Once the starter is completed, the teacher will use targeted questioning to determine whether the class has made the necessary links between the keywords. Next the lesson overview is displayed and explained to the class, as presented in Figure 3.12. In this example, pupils are told **Why** the topic is being studied and key words are shown; these are the words that pupils should be comfortable using during and by the end of lesson. There are also cross-curricular links with literacy and numeracy. Cross-curricular links can also be drawn with the study of logic gates and circuits in design and technology lessons. A good way of engaging the class at this point is to ask a pupil to read out the **Why** and the lesson objectives.

The success criteria for the lesson, see Figure 3.12, are often colour coded (traffic lights – Green, Amber, Red, where Green represents all pupils, Amber represents some pupils and Red represents a few pupils), to give guided progression through the lesson. An extension activity is also indicated.

Figure 3.12 Lesson overview

Why?	Success criteria
To gain an understanding of Logic Gates and Truth Tables (simplifying circuits for new technologies)	Identify the main Logic Gates and Truth Tables and explain the importance of Logic Gates (simulator)
Objectives:	Explain the relevance of Moore's Law
To learn about how computers use logic.	Focus on complex gates or exam-style questions
Keywords	**Extension**
AND OR NOT	**Review News Articles on Moore's Law**
Logic Gate, Truth Table	
Literacy focus:	
Use CAPITAL LETTERS, Punctuation	
Spell check (use spellchecker or dictionary)	
Numeracy	
Number systems – Binary	

During the lesson, videos are used to support explanations of logic gates and truth tables. This offers a different level of engagement aside from the 'teachers voice' – videos appeal to visual and auditory learners. The teacher then enforces the importance of logic gates in devices and the need for simplifying circuits. Additionally, each pupil takes part in an activity using logic gate simulator software, an example of which is https://logic.ly/demo/. Pupils are able to combine the gates and see the outputs in binary and hexadecimal formats.

As the lesson builds, the lesson plan also caters for pupils to explore more advanced gates and as such, during the simulator activity, pupils can do further exploration on their own or in pairs. Additionally, pupils work through a series of combined circuit diagram worksheets and write up the outcomes in truth table format. An example of a circuit that pupils work out is shown in Figure 3.13, combining an AND gate with a NOT gate.

Figure 3.13 Combined logic gate circuit

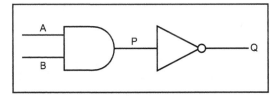

(Perhaps you can work out the output from the AND gate using the help sheet in Figure 3.14 and then work out the output from the NOT gate.)

Step 1 – Work out the output from the AND gate, the INPUTS are A and B. The OUTPUT is P

AND Gate

Input A	Input B	Output P
0	0	
0	1	
1	0	
1	1	

Step 2 – OUTPUT P from Step 1 (the AND gate) is now INPUT P into the NOT gate and the OUTPUT is Q

NOT Gate

Input P	Output Q

There is progress throughout. Weaker pupils are further supported with a logic gate and truth table help sheet, as presented in Figure 3.14. Teacher prompting and discussion takes place throughout.

Having explored logic gates, pupils are then introduced to the concept of Moore's Law. Pupils listen to a short video clip and then choose their own short questions to answer from a list provided (see Figure 3.15). This is enforcing both literacy and subject-specific language as pupils write the answers in their books and have a revision aid to return to in the future. While pupils are answering the questions in their books, the teacher is walking around and making a mental note of which questions pupils are answering; this forms the basis of targeted questioning on information given in the video. Pupils then have a paired activity to discuss what they think is the 'next step' for Moore's Law. This is designed to be a spiritual (wow) moment. Think back to SMSC.

After a short class discussion, pupils can either work individually or in small groups to read a new article on Moore's Law, for example, www.bbc.co.uk/news/technology-32335003. Each group then feeds back the main points of the article. Building in literacy activities is key as this activity re-enforces summarisation skills, encourages talking like a computer scientist and promotes discussion.

Figure 3.14 Logic gate and truth table help sheet

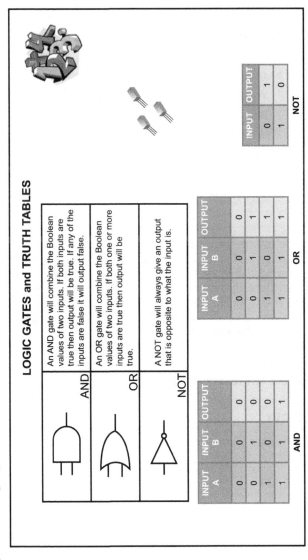

LOGIC GATES and TRUTH TABLES

AND		An AND gate will combine the Boolean values of two inputs. If both inputs are true then output will be true. If any of the inputs are false it will output false.
OR		An OR gate will combine the Boolean values of two inputs. If both one or more inputs are true then output will be true.
NOT		A NOT gate will always give an output that is opposite to what the input is.

AND

INPUT A	INPUT B	OUTPUT
0	0	0
0	1	0
1	0	0
1	1	1

OR

INPUT A	INPUT B	OUTPUT
0	0	0
0	1	1
1	0	1
1	1	1

NOT

INPUT	OUTPUT
0	1
1	0

Source: image of numerals from https://clipartfest.com/categories/view/741d79b4030f16fc84c944af86b92dec7d73d187/ math-numbers-clipart.html

Figure 3.15 Moore's Law mid-lesson discussion

Moore's Law

- Listen to the video and choose 1–2 questions to answer (1 minute)
  1. What does Moore's Law state?
  2. What is Intel?
  3. Who is Gordon Moore?

Peer Discussion – (2 minutes)

- We are on the brink of a revolution – how will we make devices smaller and slimmer?

As the lesson draws to an end, pupils are presented with the plenary in Figure 3.16 on the board. Note that pupils are answering in green pen, so when books are reviewed it is clear to see where and when pupils have reflected and drawn cross-curricular links during the lesson. The plenary offers choice, is time bonded and sentence starters are used to support and guide pupil thinking in answering the question.

Figure 3.16 Plenary activity

Plenary

Choose <u>one</u> of the following questions and in <u>green</u> pen write the answer in your book – 1 minute

1. To which other subjects can you link today's knowledge?
The other subjects to which I can link today's knowledge are...

2. What is the most important thing you have learnt today? Why is it most important?
The most important thing that I have learnt in today's lesson is.......
The reason that this is the most important is because.........

The full lesson plan for this topic is shown in Figure 3.17.

Figure 3.17 Sample short lesson plan – Logic gates and truth tables

Date:	Lesson:	Class:
Learning objective/s: To learn about Logic Gates and Truth Tables and their relevance in simplifying circuits		
Learning outcomes:		
All students:	**Most students:**	**Some students:**
• **With support**, I can create a truth table for AND, OR and NOT gates • I can simply explain the importance of simplifying circuits in relation to developing new technologies • I can create a simple circuit in a simulator • I have attempted one exam-style question	• I can create a truth table for AND, OR, NOT and XOR gates • I can explain the importance of simplifying circuits in relation to developing new technologies • I can create a circuit in a simulator • I have attempted to answer one to two exam-style questions	• I can create a truth table for AND, OR, NOT and XOR gates • I can explain in detail the importance of simplifying circuits in relation to developing new technologies • I can create a detailed circuit in a simulator • I have completed one to two exam-style questions

Brief summary of lesson[51] content:

Students are following the new National Curriculum in Computing. The focus of this lesson is Logic Gates and Truth Tables.

Afl: Targeted questioning throughout the lesson. Pupils are able to self-assess progress through a termly progress grid in the front of their books. Examples of progress grids are given in Appendix 5.

SMSC: Developed through class discussion and activities (news articles are used to get pupils to appreciate logic gates in the wider world).

(Continued)

Figure 3.17 (Continued)

> **Marking:** Pupils receive personalised feedback in their books and act upon this feedback (evident through use of green pen). The teacher keeps a mark book and end of topic tests are also used to assess knowledge.
>
> **Differentiation:** The lesson is pitched with the assumption that students will be able to grasp the basic logic gates easily, thus the worksheet has lots of complex gates and truth tables, along with expressions. Peer working will be used to support pupils. The plenary also gives choice and is supportive (examples given) on how to construct an effective answer.
>
> **Numeracy:** Pupils refer to previous knowledge gained on Binary to denary conversion and Number Systems in general.
>
> **Homework:** This is standardised across the faculty. Pupils are completing tasks from the Computational Thinking booklet. In this way flipped learning and extended learning are being used, so that students are extending their skills and gaining new knowledge.

You may well be wondering where the unplugged activity was. Unplugged methods were used in earlier lessons when pupils gained an understanding of number systems. At this stage, they are building upon their knowledge (see Figure 3.17).

> Have a practical element to every lesson. Unplugged resources are key!
>
> Steve Clarke
> Director of Computing and Curriculum Consultant
> (Secondary)

TECHNIQUES

We will now look at some of the pedagogy used in the computing classroom.

Paired programming

As the name implies, this is an activity where pupils work in pairs to write, debug and test code. This method allows for differentiation such as higher and weaker ability, challenge for higher to higher ability and support for weaker to weaker ability. The premise here is that two eyes and two heads are better than one. Pupils develop skills of teamwork, communication and respect for each other's opinions. Pupils take turns in being the 'typist of the code (driver)' or the navigator, involved in the overall planning and observing of code as it is typed in, so that there is no 'passive participation'. Problem-solving skills are greatly increased through the sharing of ideas. Remember the social part of SMSC and the mutual respect of British values.

Unplugged activities

As previously described, these are activities which do not require the use of a computer. Being aware of a variety of unplugged methods will help greatly with differentiation. These activities are excellent for encouraging teamwork and focusing on logical reasoning. Additionally, these activities do not have to be done in the classroom. On occasion, classes can be taken outside onto the school field or in a school hall to allow for more space and focus away from computers.

There are unplugged resources for almost all parts of the curriculum, unplugged databases, unplugged networks, unplugged number systems, and so on. Appendix 8 gives a reference for unplugged resources.

There are also numerous national initiatives in place to support this wonderful way of teaching computer science skills. At primary level, there is the **Barefoot Computing** program and at secondary level there is the **CAS Tenderfoot** program. Additionally, there is the **Digital Schoolhouse**[52] project by UK Interactive Entertainment (UKie) who run workshops for pupils aged 4–11. If you are new to this subject or need to 'brush up' on any computer science concepts, participate in a Barefoot workshop and then build upon your knowledge. (Note that the Barefoot programme has been adapted for Wales, Scotland and Northern Ireland.)

Computational thinking through creativity

We have looked at unplugged methods used for teaching computer science. Another medium that can be used is teaching computer science through creativity, such as through animation.[53] A benefit of this is that the results are seen straight away. This is appealing to visual learners and links to the following two statements from the computing programme of study:

> "A high-quality computing education equips pupils to use computational thinking and creativity to understand and change the world' and 'Pupils should be taught to develop their capability, creativity and knowledge in computer science, digital media and information technology."

Other ways of introducing creativity are through physical computing. Devices such as the BBC Micro:bit, Crumble, Raspberry Pi and Makey Makey boards all allow for pupils to make things and to develop their computer science knowledge along with skills such as collaboration, tinkering, problem solving and evaluation. Consider how you are incorporating, or could incorporate, creativity into your curriculum.

Numeracy

When teaching coding for the first time, introduce pupils to something that they already know, for example, drawing a square in mathematics. You could ask pupils to give instructions to a robot (a pupil could act as the robot and follow instructions, thus encouraging whole class involvement) on how to draw a square. This will encourage precise instructions and get pupils to think of angles and dimensions. This also makes use of CT skills. This activity can be used for all types of shapes. Sticking with the square example, once pupils have explained the activity as a sequence then ask them ways in which it could be made more efficient. Many pupils will say you can repeat. This can then be extended into a discussion and the acting out of different types of iteration such as repeat, repeat...until, do...while.

After pupils have understood these concepts, they can then be introduced to visual programming using a block-based programming language such as Blockey, Scratch or Snap. They can be given code for a weak group or for a higher ability group; with a small amount of explanation, they will hopefully be able to locate and snap the blocks together and run the code. Once they have done this they can then be introduced to the same activity but in a text-based programming language such as Python, using turtle graphics. (Encourage pupils to comment on their code as soon as they start using a text-based language.) This removes the need to teach visual and text-based languages separately, but rather to integrate them from the very beginning of coding activities.

Before moving onto drawing other shapes, ask pupils to recap what they know about other shapes and angles (they would have previously learnt this in Maths), such as:

- keywords – polygon, irregular polygon, and so on;

- angles on a straight line add up to 180°;

- vertically opposite angles are equal;

- pairs of corresponding angles on parallel lines are equal;

- pairs of alternate angles on parallel lines are equal;

- co-interior angles on parallel lines add up to 180°;

- parallel lines will never meet;

- the interior angles of a triangle are supplementary (add up to 180°);

- the interior angles of an n-sided polygon add to $(n - 2) \times 180°$;

- the interior angles of a regular polygon are equal;
- angles opposite the equal sides of an isosceles triangle are equal.

Having looked at pedagogy to support coding and CT concepts, we will now look at techniques that can be used to ensure pupils can handle the other rigours of the subject, such as answering exam questions and being able to write clearly and use subject-specific language. With this in mind, the computer science teacher needs to have awareness of strategies used in other subject areas which have traditionally had to prepare pupils for exams with a greater theoretical content.

Literacy

Through all key stages, written explanations need to be encouraged and emphasised, since at the end of the education journey, knowledge is examined through pupils sitting written exams in computer science[54] with a small practical element. To give pupils the experience of writing early on, one method that could be employed is in all prior key stages, to place an emphasis on literacy within computing. This requires close working with the English department or school literacy specialist. Some techniques which can be used are:

- Display and emphasise the keywords for each lesson topic; these can also be stored on a VLE.
- Ensure that pupils are using the keywords of the lesson in written or spoken discussion.
- Provide access to either online dictionaries or resources and texts such as the *BCS Glossary of Computing.*
- Incorporate literacy into starters and plenaries with activities such as:
  - Fill in the vowel.
  - Fill in the gap.

- Summarise.
- Highlight the keyword.
- Making anagrams from keywords.
- Make as many small words from one big word or words.
- Make as many subject-specific keywords from one big word.
- Spelling tests – words and meanings.
- Crossword activities.

- When analysing news articles, use the 'literature web'[55] and encourage discussion around the framework of the 'literature web'.
- Ensure pupils understand how to use connectives and support weaker pupils with sheets of connectives.
- Support weak pupils with sentence starters to help them answer questions.

For evaluations and extended writing, encourage and utilise techniques such as PETER Paragraphs and GAPS, which can assist with evaluations of products such as a computer game.

PETER Paragraphs

Point – state how you know the project or code was successful.

Evidence – support with screenshot evidence.

Technique – explain your technique, such as the use of a rollover or video for interaction or a function for reuse.

Explain – state why this would help, for example, interactive, entertaining or saves time in writing out lots of code.

Reader – how the reader, viewer or user would respond.

GAPS

Genre – explain the genre of the product.

Audience – explain to whom the product is aimed, for example, children, adults, males, females, and so on.

Purpose – state the purpose of the product, such as to entertain, inform, persuade, and so on.

Style – formal or informal? This relates to the writing style you may find on the sleeve of the product or language used with the product.

Use of these techniques greatly enhances the learning process. When you mark a piece of work you are then able to give specific feedback with points to improve.

The following shows a response from a year 9 pupil after reading teacher feedback in her book.

Thank you for the feedback. In my evaluation I am going to use PETER Paragraphs which is **P**oint, **E**vidence, **T**echnique, **E**xplain, **R**eader. Additionally, I will <u>underline</u> or make <u>keywords bold</u> as this allows the reader to see that I am using technical language.

Year 9 Pupil

THE COMPUTING CLASSROOM

One may well ask – why have a subsection just on the computing classroom? The reason for this is because computer science is both a practical and a theoretical subject. As such, the computer science teacher will need to 'manage' this environment in a slightly different way to a standard classroom. Table 3.1 shows some of the differences and issues which may arise.

Behaviour management is an issue which occurs in all aspects of teaching and may challenge a teacher when presented with additional variables in the computing classroom. You may well say that a science classroom has similar challenges to a computing classroom, as pupils have to do practical experiments. With this in mind, new teachers to the profession should liaise with teachers in other departments on how they manage pupils in their classrooms. This may help with tricky pupils.

Let's have a look at some of the differences between a standard classroom and a computing classroom.

Table 3.1 Comparison of standard and computing classroom

Standard classroom	Computing classroom
All pupils facing the teacher	Pupils can be sat facing away from the teacher
Equipment in front of pupils is usually an exercise book, a textbook and the contents of their pencil case	Equipment in front of pupils is a monitor, a base unit, a keyboard, a mouse, wires, an exercise book, the contents of their pencil case and, in some cases, also a textbook
There is no hardware or software in the classroom or additional pieces of information to remember, such as login details	Hardware may fail, software may become corrupt or just not work. Pupils may forget usernames (yes, this does happen) or passwords
Opportunities for disrupting someone else working is difficult to do without being caught	Pupils can engage in unseen low level disruption such as turning off someone else's monitor mid-work or pulling on a keyboard or mouse cable

(Continued)

Table 3.1 (Continued)

Standard classroom	Computing classroom
There is no need to learn to use other equipment	Pupils may not be familiar with the layout of a keyboard and you must factor this in when teaching
There usually is not any need for pupils to leave their seats	Classrooms have devices such as printers or scanners and pupils may get up to go to the printer. Then events such as the printer running out of paper or toner occur which is an additional factor that the teacher needs to manage. Sometimes, with pupils leaving their seats, this can lead to a pupil 'flicking' another pupil as they walk by. It is best to employ strict rules on pupils leaving their seats to go to the printer. One technique which works well, is where the teacher collects all printouts and asks a pupil to hand out the printouts. This assists in preventing any low-level disruption
There are fewer trip, fall and electrocution hazards in a standard classroom	Health and safety is always a consideration in the computing classroom. Pupils should not be drinking near to computing equipment. All cables need to be effectively tidied away by the IT department with cable ties

(Continued)

Table 3.1 (Continued)

Standard classroom	Computing classroom
There are minimised safeguarding issues arising from the digital world. However, pupils may still attempt to access the internet on their own devices	Safeguarding issues become even more paramount as pupils have access to the internet through a school computer and possibly on their own devices. Thus, teachers need to be more vigilant and use tools such as classroom management software to manage school computers and to enforce, where applicable, the school mobile phone usage policy. Remember that pupils will still attempt to get around school firewalls! Teacher vigilance needs to be high! (In Case Study 1 in Chapter 5, the teacher discusses use of classroom management software)
Pupils are directly in front of the teacher so it is easier to spot who is or isn't on task	Keeping pupils on task can be challenging due to classroom layout and not being able to see all monitors. Additionally, pupils can attempt to access material unrelated to the lesson. Again, this would be where classroom management software would be effective in being able to either see what is on each pupil's monitor or to direct content from the teacher's monitor onto the pupils monitor to ensure that all are engaged with the same material

With these differences being considered, let us look at a couple of computing classroom layouts – Figures 3.18 and 3.19.

Figure 3.18 Classroom one

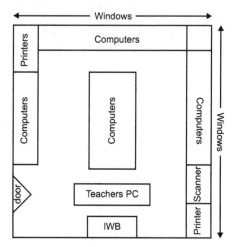

Figure 3.19 Classroom two

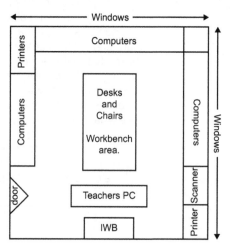

Where do you anticipate issues may arise if the teacher is standing at the IWB? What about if the teacher is standing on either the left or right hand side of the classroom? How does teacher positioning affect interaction with the pupils? This calls for awareness of the environment.

GENERAL CLASSROOM TIPS

Having gained an understanding of some of the anomalies of the computing classroom, we will look at some general tools (not previously mentioned), and a few general tips for the class and school environment.

Registers

In the classroom you are responsible for keeping an accurate register of all pupils in the room. This is part of safeguarding. The school and, by default, you, have a duty of care to your pupils. As such, if a pupil is not present in your room and you have not received prior notification from a figure of authority (do not accept the word of other pupils about absences from your lesson) then you need to immediately follow school procedure for notifying the relevant staff or attendance teams of the pupil's absence. Most registers are electronic; however, in the event of the electronic system being unavailable, a register must still be taken and this is to be done in the old-fashioned way – by hand (Figure 3.20).

Having taken the register, you are now equipped to know who is in and out of your room, to mark pupils out for toilet or medical breaks or, more importantly, be prepared for a fire drill or in the case of an emergency.

- **Fire drills and terror threats** – hopefully during your career you do not encounter any actual blazes or terror threats at your school. However, in the case of such an event, you will need to follow school policy. With fire drills, the policy is to get pupils out of the building. All pupils should leave your classroom in an

Figure 3.20 Register taken by hand

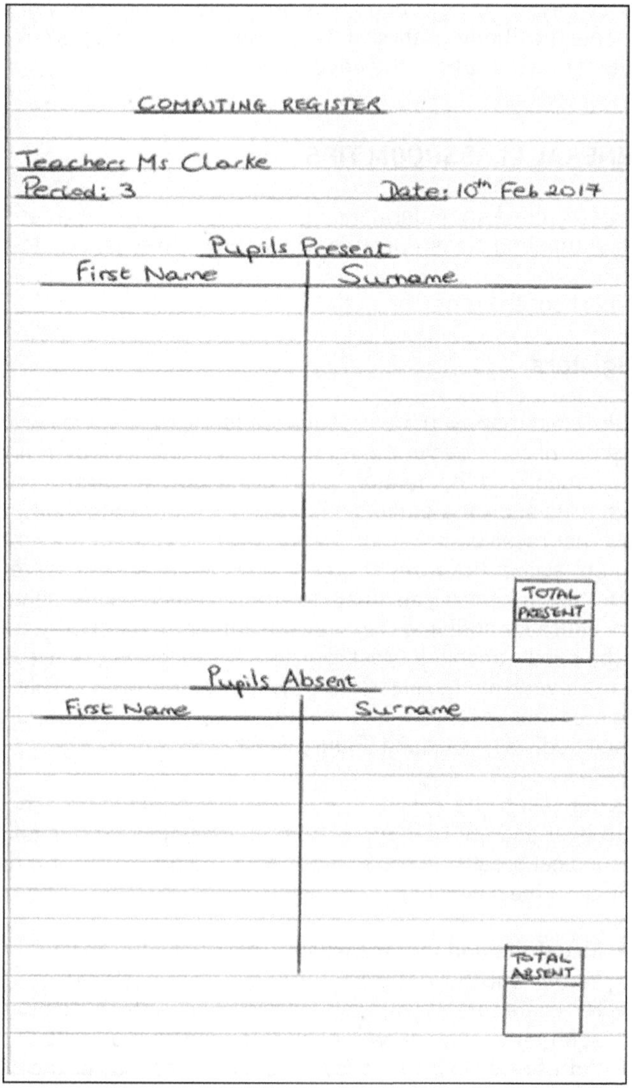

orderly fashion, leaving belongings behind. If you have taken a paper register, take this with you and lock the door behind you. Notify the nominated fire marshal that you and your class are out of the building. Pupils generally have fire assembly points on a school field or playground, where they will then line up in tutor groups in alphabetical order of surname. At this point your register will be very handy! If schools have electronic registers in place there will be local rules on how a register is taken during a fire drill. The rules on terror threats vary, so local policy needs to be followed. Information on dealing with terror threats is detailed in 'The Prevent Duty'.[56]

• **Tracking of progress** – here you will need to follow local policy at your school and the systems that they have in place for tracking progress of pupils. You will need to demonstrate progress, in lessons, from lesson to lesson and across an academic year. Pupils will need to be working at their target grade level (think back to Chapter 1 and earlier in this chapter when Progress and Attainment 8 were discussed); target grades are the attainment that each pupil is expected to achieve at the end of their school journey in year 11. So, in year 7 (key stage 3), a pupil would be expected to be producing work of sufficient quality to remain on a trajectory for achieving their target grade in year 11 (key stage 4). Remember also that we have previously looked at tools which capture progress and understanding, with many generating data which can then be linked into the school reporting system. Where pupils are not making progress, you will also need to liaise with others in your department and look at intervention strategies to ensure that pupils progress and achieve. You will also hear the word 'APP' (Assessing Pupil Progress); this simply means the way in which the department assesses progress. One such way is by progress grids[57] in pupil books, which pupils can tick off as a way of self-assessing topics.

- **Thank your class** – at the end of each lesson when your class is lined up ready to be dismissed (in an orderly fashion) thank them for their work and effort. Everyone likes to be praised. If you hadn't previously done so during the lesson, give them your top moments during the lesson and, if time allows, tell them what they will do next lesson. Tell them how excited you are to be teaching a topic such as robotics, that it is an area of personal interest. They will appreciate it, as they will want to know what you know and come back next lesson wanting more!

- **Report writing** – schools are legally required to report to parents once per year on their child's progress. This will usually take the form of a school report. Here you will need to follow the school's guidelines for report writing. Schools also send home termly progress updates either electronically or on paper. An example of an end of year report is presented in Figure 3.21. You will note from accurate register taking that these data then feed directly into the report giving data on attendance. Within the teacher comments box the teacher will usually set a target for the pupil in that subject. The target column is colour coded[58] – green, amber, red to give a visual indication of the pupil's progress.

DIVERSITY AND INCLUSION IN THE COMPUTING CLASSROOM

All subjects on the English National Curriculum including computing should be accessible to all groups of pupils. However, there are some challenges faced in the classroom. There are a few groups of pupils who nationally do not take up the subject in expected numbers, are under-represented or do not progress as well as their peers. These groups are shown in Figure 3.22.

Figure 3.21 End of year report

School Logo			Year 7 Report July 2017 J.Bloggs

Name		Possible Attendance	
Tutor Group		Actual Attendance	
Lates		Unauthorised Absence	

Subject	Target	Teacher Comment
Art		
Computer Science		
English		
Maths		
Music		
Physical Education		
Science		

Tutor Comment

Head of Year Comment

Head teacher Comment

School address and contact details

Figure 3.22 Diversity and inclusion

Diversity	Inclusion
Gender – for example, female pupils	Special Education Needs (SEN)
Gifted and Talented/More Able	English as an Additional Language (EAL)
Pupils in the pupil premium[59] category	
Ethnicity – for example, black and Asian pupils	
Socio-economic – for example, white working class boys or families who have never gone to university	
LGBT pupils	
Disabled pupils – be this a physical or visual impairment	

Source: adapted from classification by #include http://casinclude.org.uk

When standing in front of a new class for the very first time, a useful awareness activity is to look at the class and be aware of your own perceptions – conscious and unconscious bias. It is worth thinking what leads to these conclusions? We will now examine these groups and look at ways of bridging the gaps in class.

Diversity

- **Gender** – the first thing here is to know your pupils. Find out what all pupils in the class, including the girls, would like to do as a career and what they do on their mobile devices – this will provide a hook into their interests and help you to relate classroom activities. Ask them the about the ways in which they use computing devices socially. Once the 'hook' is found, then show them the relevance of what is being taught to their lives. So, if stereotypically, a girl says, 'I am going to be a nail technician and I don't need computers' then explain that learning about spreadsheets will help with invoicing clients, learning about websites will help to promote their business and that an algorithm is in use when doing a nail procedure or hairdressing treatment in order to get the desired result. This same thinking can be applied to a boy, who says 'I am going to be a builder or fisherman and don't need this subject'. The building trade has lots of applications for computing such as Computer Aided Design (CAD) and the fishing industry makes use of computing through Global Positioning Systems (GPS), sonar, wireless communications and other technologies. Through this explanation, pupils should see that computing is relevant to all occupations.

There are daily news headlines about the lack of numbers of females taking GCSE and A-level computer science. This is not only a school issue it is a part of a wider cultural issue. There are lots of women using technology but most technology is made by men. There is a perception that only geeks or nerds do computer science. Dispel this myth by having wall displays that positively promote women. In the school library or on the VLE[60] include books such as the BCS *Women in IT – Inspiring the Next Generation* ebook.[61] Encourage pupils to look at the work of groups such as the BCS Women's group. This will be beneficial to their professional and corporate lives in the future.

Other ways of addressing the gender imbalance is for all pupils to celebrate 'Ada Lovelace Day' across the school. This will allow for cross-curricular links as this day is usually celebrated as part of celebrating women in STEAM subjects. All pupils will then learn about famous women in science such as Marie Curie. This could provide an opportunity for writing activities with the English department or drawing activities with the art department. Further ways of bringing the contributions of women in IT to the fore are as a part of International Women's Day. This can also be celebrated as a whole-school cross-curricular activity.

Enrichment activities (trips) to places of computing interest such as Bletchley Park are also useful, as are related homework activities – encourage all pupils to find out about the 'Women of Bletchley Park' and their crucial involvement in code breaking.

- **Pupils in the pupil premium category, Gifted and Talented or More Able, ethnicity** – another way of closing such gaps is to have special days which focus on pupils in these groups. For example, workshops for girls or boys in the pupil premium. In this way, a teacher and the school will be able to demonstrate that measures are being taken to address underachievement by pupils in this category. The same measures can be taken for Gifted and Talented or More Able pupils. For pupils of ethnic groups such as black or Asian pupils, have a look around the department and classrooms, consider whether pupils see anyone that is representative of them in a positive way. If this is not the case, then this is an area that needs to be addressed.

- **Socio-economic groups, for example, white working class boys** – currently this group of pupils is underachieving nationally, with many boys stereotypically simply wishing for a 'career in football'. This group will also benefit from positive re-enforcement of what they can achieve and from guest speakers. Knowing your pupils works here again; for example, if teaching about spreadsheets, the football scores can be shown in a spreadsheet and the pupils should be very quickly able to work out the number of points based upon 3 for a win, 1 for a draw or 0 for a loss and work out who is at the top of the table and the bottom. A variety of skills would be called on for this activity: mathematical and sorting skills. This activity can be done without a computer. It is a way of engaging with the pupils. An example of a football premier league table is set out in Figure 3.23.

STANDARDS, TOOLS, METHODS AND TECHNIQUES

Figure 3.23 Premier League table

Position	Team	P	W	D	L	F	A	GD	Pts
1	Chelsea	25	19	3	3	52	18	34	60
2	Manchester City	25	16	4	5	51	29	22	52
3	Tottenham Hotspur	25	14	8	3	46	18	28	50
4	Arsenal	25	15	5	5	54	28	26	50
5	Liverpool	25	14	7	4	54	30	24	49
6	Manchester United	25	13	9	3	38	21	17	48
7	Everton	25	11	8	6	40	27	13	41
8	West Bromwich Albion	25	10	7	8	34	31	3	37
9	Stoke City	25	8	8	9	30	36	−6	32
10	West Ham United	25	9	5	11	34	43	−9	32

Source: www.bbc.co.uk/sport/football/premier-league/table (accessed 19 February 2017)

This activity can be applied equally to other sports. A CT term such as Decomposition can be applied here to decompose 'What is the game of football?' Another way in is, for example, what happens if a player is in the 'off side position'? Pupils will be able to say the game is stopped and then the referee awards an indirect free kick where the offence occurred. Another activity could be a discussion on the use of 'Big Data' to analyse the performance of a footballer or other sports person, around data collected by cameras, sensors, wearables and how these can be used to track and improve performance. Activities such as this assist pupils in reasoning and explaining what has happened. These are key computing points.

- **Sexual orientation** – another group of pupils to consider are those that fall into the 'invisible' category.

Groups such as ethnicity and physical disability are easier to see; however, there are groups of pupils such as Lesbian, Gay, Bisexual, Transgender (LGBT) pupils who also need to be feel safe and included within the school environment whether they are **'out'** or not. Many pupils come from LGBT families, so even if they do not identify as LGBT, they also have a need to see and hear positive representation in the classroom and school environment. It would be wise to develop using non-gendered language in the classroom, thus making for a diverse and inclusive environment. Avoid stereotypes such as pink for girls and blue for boys. Allow all pupils to choose their own colours in activities which require resources such as marking pens, coloured paper, and so on. During LGBT history month (February), you could draw the attention of the class to campaigns run by organisations such as BCS – 'OUTinSTEM heroes' which features past and present LGBT heroes in technology, from Alan Turing to modern day heroes.

Inclusion

- **Special Education Needs (SEN) pupils and disabled pupils** – there is a common stereotype that the new computing curriculum is aimed at pupils who are higher ability or good at mathematics. Remember, this is a curriculum for every child. Your role as a teacher is to ensure that all pupils progress and attain their best. As such, the teacher will need to differentiate accordingly to ensure that the classroom is inclusive. For pupils of weaker ability or who have more needs (physical disability, literacy, numeracy, dyslexia, dyscalculia, visual impairment, auditory impairment, emotional or social interaction, and so on) who struggle to grasp and develop computer science skills and knowledge in line with their peers, a variety of different techniques need to be used. There should be lots of scaffolding work, with images and voice clips, to support their learning. For a visually challenged pupil, increasing the font size on the screen would be a starting point. For all pupils, access to videos and MOOCs[62] will help to promote and re-enforce the learning process beyond the classroom. Use of physical computing devices (such as the Raspberry Pi, Crumbles or BBC Microbit) to illustrate concepts is also key. Additionally, use of assistive technologies such as text to speech converters (screen readers) and magnifier tools greatly assists, depending on the need of the pupil.

Unplugged activities are also extremely important as pupils need to understand computer science concepts before going onto a computer and learning to program. For example, using everyday things to which the pupil can relate to explain CT terms such as algorithms and abstraction is critical. Sorting and searching activities can be done in the classroom through dance, sorting boxes, books and many other items to illustrate sorting and searching algorithms. The same for sequencing, selecting and repeating concepts.

Whether working in a special or mainstream school, one way of raising pupil awareness is to ask pupils to find topical news articles on people with SEN in technology, such as people on the autistic spectrum being recruited to work for major technology companies such as Microsoft and Hewlett Packard. Ask pupils to find out what skills these companies desire.

Another way of raising awareness is, when teaching websites or using websites, to point out tools and features such as accessibility[63] settings. Most pupils have a mobile device, depending on the school policy on mobile devices, ask pupils to have a look at their devices and explore the accessibility functions, find out how they work. Point out that there are visible and invisible disabilities; the pupil wearing contact lenses or who is colour blind has a need, but this is not immediately known.

For all SEN pupils, the teacher needs to work with the SEN department and to be aware of strategies for engagement and progression in that pupil's Individual Education Plan (IEP)[64]/Education Healthcare Plan (EHCP). In the case studies in Chapter 5, you will notice that some schools have a large percentage of SEN pupils. This is a reality and new entrants into the profession must be aware of such challenges.

- **English as an Additional Language (EAL)** – when working with EAL pupils, follow the school EAL policy, which may include strategies such as seating EAL pupils in groups or next to pupils where they will hear the best use of language, have foreign language dictionaries in the classroom as well as approved online translation tools, and using simple language to explain concepts. To make an EAL pupil feel welcome, perhaps learn to say 'good morning', 'goodbye' and 'well done' in their language. This goes a long way towards including everyone.

It is worth noting that some teachers may be in environments in which they have no exposure to pupils from any of these categories. However, it is prudent to bear in mind that the pupils in your classroom are being prepared to function in our society and the public is diverse; as such, wall displays, guest speakers and raising awareness is important. Remember with all pupils, including those in these categories, it is the job of the teacher to assist with instilling pride and positive attitudes, which is why it is so important that difference is celebrated. The concept of 'British Values'[65] is fully on the school curriculum across all subjects and this is a perfect example of promoting mutual respect and tolerance.

Most schools have 'end of term' and 'end of year' achievement assemblies or ceremonies. To show that all achieve, it is wise to celebrate the achievements for at least one pupil from each of the groups above in addition to the rest of the school population. This will make the pupils subliminally realise that all can achieve and all deserve respect. Additionally, if staff fall into any of the groups mentioned and are happy to have information shared about them then this should be celebrated so that pupils have a real living role model in front of them.

With all pupils, one of the best strategies for closing academic gaps is effective feedback on their work and ensuring that pupils act upon that feedback. This is where effective marking comes into play, which directs the pupil on how to progress and to plan how they will achieve their targets within computer science. Pupils will then be able to reflect on their learning journey. At this point it would be wise to do further reading into the work of the Education Endowment Foundation (EEF)[66] who have resources such as a toolkit of intervention strategies. Another source for further reading is the Sutton Trust.[67] This is an excellent website to read about the reasons behind these gaps, how they are changing and recommendations for closing them.

As we conclude this section it is also worth noting that CAS has a group that focuses on diversity and the inclusive classroom called #include which has resources and further reading links. The aims of #include are in Figure 3.24.

Figure 3.24 Aims of #include

- To help teachers seeking to promote inclusion in computing and ICT lessons, focusing on the issues of gender, ethnicity, SEN, disability and socio-economic groups.
- To run high quality events for teachers seeking to promote inclusion and for students who may not otherwise have an opportunity to experience computer science.
- To provide access to high quality classroom resources that will help promote diversity and inclusion.
- To act as a point of contact between teachers and industry so that we can work together to achieve these goals.

There is also research by the University of Roehampton into 'Computing and Identity', which is detailed in 'The Roehampton Annual Computing Education Report 2015',[68] which provides a thought provoking read.

Across the case studies in Chapter 5, you will find teacher discussion on creating a diverse and inclusive classroom. Remember that teaching is about getting the best from everyone. The following quote sums this up.

> Overall, I believe that techniques that are good for subsets of students are good for ALL students.
>
> Chris Sharples
> Head of Computing (Secondary)

DAILY INTERACTION

Having explored what we are going to teach and managing the learning environment, we will now examine the school day in detail. In the vast majority of schools the school week is Monday to Friday. There are a few exceptions to this rule, such as independent schools. If there are any variations in a state school, it would be wise to read your contract carefully and refer to the 'School teachers pay and conditions' guidance document.[69] Schools are legally required to be open 195 days per year and a full-time teacher is expected to be available to work for 190 of these days and the other five are usually made up with INSET[70] days.

At the start of each academic year, staff are issued with their timetable for that academic year. The timetable shows the classes and subjects to be taught, breaks, lunchtime, any duty rota and any Planning, Preparation and Assessment (PPA) time. PPA time is non-pupil contact time for teachers to do as the words say: plan, prepare and assess. This is a statutory right for all teachers.

Analysis of secondary timetable example

Table 3.2 shows an example timetable for a full-time secondary teacher with no additional responsibilities. This is based on a possible 25 slots per week, each slot being one hour in duration. The teacher teaches 21 hours per week. This is contact time with the pupils. This timetable is across two different key stages and across a variety of sets,[71] with two hours' PPA time and an additional two hours that are unallocated; these are discretionary. The timetable for a Newly Qualified Teacher (NQT) will be 10 per cent less.

The school week starts off in this example with a short staff meeting on Monday morning. These usually take place in the staffroom and are chaired by the head teacher or other member of the SLT. They tend to be short to give the staff body information such as visits from external visitors, information on pupils such as a major hospitalisation, broken leg, and so on, a quick roundup of any staff who may be offsite or any other business. The staff meeting is sometimes the only time during the week where you get to see colleagues from other departments.

On this timetable, you may well ask what happens during the unallocated slots. The answer to this is twofold. This is similar to PPA time (use your time wisely!) and on occasion, the school may ask you to 'cover'. A cover involves taking a lesson for a colleague who is sick, offsite, in a meeting or for other reasons which means that they cannot take their own timetabled lesson. Cover lessons are not necessarily within your own subject area.[72] They can and usually are for any other subject that is taught in the school. Thus, you may find yourself covering a lesson in drama, music, art, geography, history, modern foreign languages (MFL), maths, English, science, food technology, technology or another department!

Covers are always interesting! They call on your skills of being adaptable. Sometimes, you may have never taught the class that you have to cover, so you are almost back to day one of teaching without knowing names and may have a few aspects

Table 3.2 Example secondary weekly timetable

	Monday	Tuesday	Wednesday	Thursday	Friday
	Staff meeting				
	Tutor time	Tutor time assembly	Tutor time	Tutor time	Tutor time assembly
Period 1	Year 7 – set 1	Year 10 – GCSE computer science	Year 11 – GCSE computer science	PPA	Year 9 – set 1
Period 2	Year 8 – set 2	Year 10 – GCSE computer science	Year 9 – set 3	Year 9 – set 2	Year 9 – set 2
	B	R	E (Break Duty)	A	K
Period 3	PPA	Year 7 – set 3	Year 9 – set 1	Year 11 – GCSE computer science	Year 8 – set 4
Period 4	Year 9 – set 1	Year 7 – set 2		Year 11 – GCSE computer science	Year 8 – set 1
	L	U	N	C	H
Period 5	Year 7 – set 4	Year 10 – GCSE computer science		Year 9 – set 4	Year 8 – set 3
Afterschool	CPD	Catch-up and intervention	Detentions and intervention	Computing club	

of behaviour management to manage, a different room layout and trying to deliver a lesson that is not in your comfort zone. Thankfully most schools avoid putting their regular staff on cover and tend to employ 'cover supervisors' who fulfil this role when colleagues cannot take their own class. However, all teachers will at some point do a cover or covers. It is surprising what you will learn about other subject areas and about the pupils when you teach them in another subject area.

On the timetable, you will notice that the day starts with tutor time, which is time to meet with your tutor group.[73] Tutor time is usually about 20–30 minutes in duration. Many schools have a tutor time programme. During tutor time, you will be expected to deliver a programme to your tutor group. Tutor programmes tend to have a social element to them, so that pupils learn to bond with each other (remember SMSC). During tutor activities, you get to know your tutor group very well. For many pupils, you will become a constant and trusted person in their lives. For some pupils, you may be the only constant in their lives every morning. Do not underestimate the power of tutor time in addition to lesson time! Examples of activities that tutor groups undertake are quizzes, planning for tutor group assemblies, participating in 'in-school' competitions, anti-bullying initiatives, drug awareness, managing stress workshops, analysing the local or general election, analysing the news, and so on. Tutor time is very varied.

A few times during the week tutor time is given over to assemblies. Assemblies are taken at least once per week by a member of the school's SLT or by heads of year. On other occasions, assembly time may be given over to external speakers or used for in-school celebrations. Examples of external speakers may be talks from the local fire brigade, local police, local churches, local youth centres, and so on, and generally link to the material being covered in the tutor programme. In some schools, at least annually, a tutor group will need to deliver an assembly to the rest of their year group. This is good as a bonding experience for the pupils in the year group; however, this can be daunting for the teacher and for some pupils. Themes for such assemblies are decided with the school.

In secondary schools, year 11 leave school in the summer term, usually May onwards. Teachers tend to have 'year 11 free time', however, this is not 'free' time and teachers can find themselves reallocated to teach or cover other classes or, in many schools, are expected to use the time to plan for the coming academic year. Traditionally, school trips are built into this time. In primary schools, the time after SATs is when pupils have activities to prepare them for secondary school.

On Wednesday, you will notice 'break duty' is scheduled; this is a contractual duty. Teachers are legally obliged to do a duty outside of their subject knowledge lesson time. Break duty is about 15 to 20 minutes long and can be undertaken anywhere within the school, for example, in the playground, main hall, corridors, and so on. The reason for this is that pupils need to be kept safe not only in the classroom but also out of class. Being on duty, you will need to keep an eye and ear out for isolated pupils or those struggling to fit in, unhealthy 'friendship' groups, pupils smoking, pupils drinking alcohol, using foul language, pupils climbing trees or fences and doing themselves injury, directly kicking balls at each other, tripping each other up, pupil fights, and so on. Most of these situations do not occur on a daily basis, but nevertheless they do occur and, as such, being on break duty means being vigilant. On the many days when the school population is working along nicely and if on a break duty outside, it is a perfect time for fresh air and to enjoy the sunshine or crisp winter weather.

On this timetable, you will notice that after period 5, there are additional events after school. For example, on Monday, there is CPD time. CPD in this instance is not necessarily subject-related, but linked to wider teaching and school life. Examples of CPD events are health and safety awareness, fire safety awareness, effective ways of marking, formative assessment strategies, and so on. On Tuesday and Wednesday, there are catch-up and intervention sessions. Catch-up is for pupils who have fallen behind in their classwork and this can be for a variety of reasons, such as missed lessons through illness or struggling with the taught material. Within your department, there will be local policy on how to manage catch-up sessions.

Intervention sessions are usually for pupils who are failing to make the required progress in your subject; the tendency here is to focus on those areas in which the pupil is having difficulty and work on those areas. In a secondary school this may be to focus on exam questions around a certain topic or in primary school this may be to improve reading and comprehension (although this can happen at secondary also). Of course, you may well have a lot of support material on the VLE, so this would be very helpful to you and the pupil at this point; however, teaching is a 'people business' and sometimes targeted intervention sessions are the only way to ensure that some pupils progress and achieve.

On Wednesday, in this example, there are detentions[74] and after school catch-up; this could be up to one hour after school. Detentions could be for pupils who have failed to complete homework, have been disrespectful to you during lessons, have not completed class work, have not brought the correct equipment to your lesson and other reasons. With detentions, you will need to follow your school's detention policy.

Thursday's afterschool session is for enrichment activity. This could be anything from a robotics club or film club to an animation club, coding club, and so on. Afterschool clubs tend to be about an hour long.

At certain times of year, the school will host events which will take you through to about 8.00 p.m. or 9.00 p.m.; such events are options[75] evenings, open evenings, parents' evenings. You will be pleased to hear that the afterschool events are suspended on these occasions to allow setup time for these other events. On some days, the school day is very long. Add into this a termly lesson observation, which will fall on a busy week!

It is worth noting that many secondary schools work on a two-week timetable, such as week A and week B or week 1 and week 2. This means that you will have a timetable for week 1 and another for week 2. The reasons for this are many, but essentially it allows for a greater offering of subjects and to avoid certain days becoming 'tedious' as every other week is different. With primary schools the same timetable applies from week to week.

Having taken you through the school week, you may now have noticed that being a teacher is very busy! In such a busy time, you will learn two things to get you through: resilience and a sense of humour! The quote that follows gives one teacher's view of starting a teaching position.

> Upon taking up my post, I was the department. It took a few months to settle into post and to let my personality shine through into my teaching.
>
> Steve Clarke
> Director of Computing and
> Curriculum Consultant (Secondary)

Analysis of primary timetable example

Table 3.3 shows an example timetable for a full-time primary teacher with no additional responsibilities.

In this example, you will notice that the teacher has PPA time on a Friday. During this time, the class will be taken by externally-hired staff. Afterschool activities also happen at primary level and take place after 3.15 p.m.; these can be run by school teachers or by external staff.

So far, the timetable is showing your interaction with pupils and perhaps a teaching assistant in some classes. However, there are a few other colleagues who have so far not been mentioned in this book, these are:

- **Site staff** (for example, caretaker, cleaner) – essential in knowing who to speak to for putting up things such as display boards, replacing blown light bulbs in the classroom, removing broken chairs, desks, work benches, cleaning up mess such as spillages in corridors, and so on.

Table 3.3 Example primary weekly timetable – Year 2

	Monday	Tuesday	Wednesday	Thursday	Friday
8.45 a.m. to 9.10 a.m.	Registration, silent reading, handwriting				
9.10 a.m. to 9.30 a.m.	Assemblies – (including values and sharing)				
9.30 a.m. to 10.30 a.m.	Maths	Science	Maths	English	Physical Education (PPA)
	BREAK				
10.45 a.m. to 11.45 a.m.	English	Maths	English	Maths	Music (PPA)
	LUNCHTIME				
12.45 p.m. to 13.10 p.m.	Phonics	Guided Reading	Spellings	Phonics	Spellings (PPA)
13.10 p.m. to 14.00 p.m.	History	English	Physical Education	Science	Religious Education
	BREAK				
14.10 p.m. to 15.15 p.m.	Art	Computing	Geography	Extended Writing	Music
15.00 p.m. to 15.15 p.m.	Tidy up, storytime, prepare to go home				

- **IT technicians**[76] – these are the technical staff who are responsible for the running of the school network, loading of new software, retrieving work that a pupil has mistakenly deleted (usually on the same day it is due! A sense of humour is required at such a point), managing pupil passwords, replacing broken computer equipment, and so on.

- **School receptionist** – a vital person(s), the receptionist will see and be aware of everyone who walks into the school. This is very useful when you have a package delivered and it doesn't make it to your classroom and 'no one knows where it is' (sense of humour required again). The receptionist will be your go to person in such a situation.

- **School librarian** – all schools have an area which is generally referred to as the Learning Resource Centre (LRC) or library. The LRC will hold textbooks and provide computer access for pupils outside of class time. Good relationships with the LRC will help to ensure computing book titles are stocked in the library, data on popularity of resources accessed and borrowed will be available to you easily and quickly. Providing the LRC staff with a copy of your schemes of work and letting them know what the pupils may be requesting is a good idea for 360-degree support for pupils.

> All schools are not the same. The routines, timings and structure can be hugely different.
>
> Jayne Fenton-Hall
> Head of IT and Computing (Secondary)

PROMOTING YOUR SUBJECT

One of the things that a teacher will do on a daily basis is promote their subject so that pupils are continually seeing the relevance of computing not just in the teacher's classroom but the relevance of it across the curriculum. Practical ways of promoting your subject which are quick wins with the pupils and at events such as open evenings and options evenings are:

- **Wall displays** – these should be relevant and topical, and should be in classrooms and on corridors leading up to classrooms in the computing department. Ideas for displays are:

  - **Computing hall of fame** – featuring people who have made positive and long lasting impacts in the field of computing and the digital world.

  - **Women in IT** – featuring influential women in the industry past and present.

  - **Computer-animated films** – films made entirely through computer generated imagery (CGI) such as *Frozen.*

  - **Computer films** – which feature a computer-related story such as *Robots.*

  - **Industry-related logos** – to help pupils with recognising that the computer industry is integral to their lives.

  - **'Jobs in IT' or 'Jobs which use IT'** – this emphasises the relevance of the subject to all jobs.

  - **LGBT heroes** – this is a part of diversity and could be part of a changing display and be shown during LGBT history month every February.

  - **Topic-specific displays** – this could feature topics such as cybersecurity, the Internet of Things, Big Data, 3D printing, green IT, cloud computing, and so on.

  The idea here is to move away from traditional 'uninteresting displays' such as hardware, software, network topologies and to show computer science in a wider sense.

- **Computing Voice group** – as this is still a relatively new subject, getting an interested group of pupils across the school body or key stages to meet termly to discuss computing within the school will give rise to information on what pupils find of interest. Additionally, the group will be a focus for pupils who have strong computing interests and it will serve as a forum in which they develop. They can be further inspired by specialist workshops for specific interests and encouraged to enter national competitions for specific interest. A bonus of participating in such a group could be that pupils have a badge that they wear with words like 'Computing Champion' or 'Computing Voice'. Members of this group if they wish can also feed information back to their year groups or tutor groups about what is discussed at Computing Voice meetings, in terms of how computing will be improved or grown across the school. Some schools also have 'Digital Leaders', who are pupils that fulfil a similar role and take an interest in computing (Case Study 4 in Chapter 5 has mention of Digital Leaders).

- **Books in the LRC or school library** – ensure that the LRC is well stocked with computing-related literature such as magazines and books. Magazines should be specialist magazines such as those on operating systems and mobile devices not found in school. Book examples could be those that feature biographies of famous people in computing, the *BCS Glossary of Computing*, resource pamphlets such as those by CS4FN. These are just a few starter ideas to allow for pupils to access computing in their own time.

- **SMSC or British Values display** – this can feature imagery for areas such as file sharing, plagiarism, snooping, organised religion, replacing bibles (or other holy books) with digital devices in places of worship, priests (or other religious leaders) reading from digital devices instead of traditional holy books, censorship, the digital divide and many more. Along with the imagery should be a thought-provoking caption or a question which generates discussion.

- **School newsletter** – most schools have a termly newsletter which reaches a very wide audience: pupils, parents, the local community and beyond. Newsletters are in the public domain and can assist greatly with raising the profile of your school within the community. Examples of features for the school newsletter are details of school trips, special event days such as celebrating 'Safer Internet Day' or 'Computer Science Education Week' or 'Code Week', along with quotes from pupils on what they gained from the event. There could be a feature for upcoming afterschool clubs. Some schools have in-house book clubs; if this is the case speak with the school librarian and have a computing-related book feature on the book club list. This is all good advertising for the subject. Additionally, if your school is part of the NoE, a lead school or a CAS Hub, then this detail can feature in the school newsletter.

- **Trips** – try to organise school trips that cater for either specific year groups or a cross section of pupils. Examples of places are:

  - Bletchley Park.
  - The National Museum of Computing.
  - Science Museum.
  - Telegraph Museum.
  - Royal Signals Museum.
  - Goonhilly Earth Station.

  A more comprehensive list can be found at – http://community.computingatschool.org.uk/resources/1823

  Examples of enrichment could range from trips to local museums which have computing displays and also run computing-focused workshops, trips to the cinema to see computing-related films, robotics events and cross-curricular fairs with subjects such as science which also feature computing; an example of this is the 'Big Bang Fair'.

It would be wise to point out at this point that when organising a school trip, teachers are tasked with carrying out a risk assessment before the trip can take place. You will need to follow in-house guidance on required paperwork to complete and gain parental permission to take pupils offsite. Costings need to be made, transport will need to be booked and provision made for lunches and breaks. Staffing will also need to be considered for the correct staff to pupil ratio and additional staff may be required for vulnerable pupils. Some of the points which feature on a risk assessment are making adequate provision for staff and pupils to travel to and from the venue, what to do in case of a fire or other evacuation situation at the venue and managing medical incidents. Justification of the value of the trip to pupils will also need to be given. When planning a school trip do this long in advance of the event, at least a few terms, to ensure that everything is in order and all interested parties are informed.

- **National events and competitions** – there are many annual national events and competitions in which your pupils should be encouraged to participate. Some examples of events are:

  - **The University of Manchester animation competition** for primary and secondary pupils.

  - **3dami** – who run a residential competition to create and develop a 3D animated film in a week, aimed at secondary pupils.

  - **Teentech** – who run awards for STEM subjects to create innovations to benefit society, aimed at secondary pupils.

  - **Cybersecurity competitions** – which tend to focus on code breaking and competing against others to develop ways to protect against security threats, aimed at primary and secondary pupils.

  - **Bebras** – a series of CT challenges. Aimed at primary and secondary pupils.

These are just a few events; there is an up-to-date list of events and competitions available on the CAS website – http://community.computingatschool.org.uk/resources/43

- **Cross-curricular computing** – organise cross-curricular computing projects with the technology department (secondary) for example, for activities such as building seven segment[77] displays in technology and learning how they work in computer science. Pupils will then have their own seven segment display to take home and of course they would have understood the binary behind the display. Also with the tech department, team up on projects that can use a Crumble[78] (primary), in tech pupils learn about the circuits and in computer science they program the Crumble. There is also scope for collaboration with the music department at key stages 1–3, such as coding the compositions studied in music in a computer science lesson, in a visual programming language such as Scratch. This does not require the teacher to know music as the pupils will know the notes (help sheets will provide support for those with additional needs). Pupils will love this and wish to explore making all sorts of music; in doing so they then start taking themselves beyond the classroom and even showing off at home! As previously mentioned, team up with the maths department and English departments. Links can also be made with science and computers can be used to analyse data collected. The possibilities for cross-curricular activity are abundant.

- **Careers day** – one way of boosting the importance of computer science in all jobs is to collaborate with the school careers person at secondary school and organise guest speakers from a variety of industries to visit as part of a careers fair to speak to the pupils about ways in which their subject knowledge is used in the real world. For example, inviting in a nurse or doctor, a software engineer, a newspaper editor, a research scientist or a games developer would provide for showing wide usage of computing skills. Such an event can also be supported by local computer companies. This can also be tailored to a primary school who may have a professions day, to look at how computers help specific jobs to which the pupils can easily relate.

- **Makerspace** – this is an area set aside for pupils to get together and have fun exploring new software and hardware. Makerspaces support inquiry-based flipped learning. Pupils will have the opportunity to investigate topics on their own and feed their findings back to the class. There is also great potential for cross-curricular projects and in-school competitions as the space will give pupils access to all that is required for their project. Getting pupils from a 'Computing Voice' or 'Digital Leaders' group involved in creating the space and the aims will assist in selling computer science.

4 CAREER PROGRESSION AND RELATED ROLES

This chapter outlines the qualifications and experience required to be a teacher and describes the pay scales in the teaching profession. Insight on career progression paths within and out of the school environment are covered and advice is offered on where to find a teaching job and on places to recruit teachers.

QUALIFICATIONS AND EXPERIENCE REQUIRED

Having read through this book, and noted in Chapter 2 the qualifications and training in the person specification of the job adverts, we will now develop this and look at qualifications and experience required in greater detail.

What now follows is the most up-to-date guidance on becoming a teacher from the DfE (Figure 4.1).

Figure 4.1 Teacher qualification requirements

GCSE requirement

If you want to train to teach, you will need to demonstrate:

A standard equivalent to a GCSE grade C or grade 4 in Mathematics and English to teach at secondary level

(Continued)

Figure 4.1 (Continued)

A standard equivalent to a GCSE grade C/grade 4 in Mathematics and English and a science subject to teach at primary level

Your training provider will make the final decision on whether you meet this entry criteria – if you don't, they may ask you to sit a GCSE equivalency test, or offer other evidence to demonstrate your attainment

Source: https://getintoteaching.education.gov.uk/eligibility-for-teacher-training

Additionally, a UK degree is required; at secondary level this is generally a subject-specific degree. On top of the degree you will need to gain Qualified Teacher Status (QTS). Depending upon the route you take into teaching, you may have a degree with QTS or you may have to add a QTS-only route to your degree. If you don't have a degree you will need to follow an approved university undergraduate course that includes QTS. For overseas trained teachers, you will need to contact an approved training provider to check for eligibility. If you do not have a computer science, computing or IT degree or need to refresh your knowledge, then prior to undertaking teacher training, you will also need to complete a Subject Knowledge Enhancement[79] (SKE) course.

With regard to experience this depends on your age and what you have gathered in life prior to entering the teaching profession. All people- or customer-focused activity will assist in being a teacher and indeed all life experiences. Remember teaching is a people-centred job! Also, think back to the attributes, knowledge and skills discussed in Chapter 2. It would also be a good idea to gain work experience[80] in a school before committing to a teaching programme.

PAY SCALES

Qualified teachers enter the teaching profession on a pay scale. This pay scale is called the 'Main Pay Scale' (MPS). The pay ranges are revised annually. There are six points on the pay scale between min and max, starting at MPS1 up to MPS6. If a teacher is performing well, they advance one point up the main pay scale each year. Upon reaching the end of the MPS, teachers can then go through what is called Threshold and move onto the Upper Pay Scale (UPS). There are three levels at UPS, which start at UPS1 through to UPS3. Pay varies depending upon the part of the country in which you work. Table 4.1 illustrates the differences in the pay scales.

Table 4.1 Teacher salary ranges (2017)

	England and Wales excluding London and fringe	Inner London	Outer London	London fringe
Max	£33,160	£38,241	£36,906	£34,249
Min	£22,467	£28,098	£26,139	£23,547

Source: https://getintoteaching.education.gov.uk/funding-and-salary/teacher-salaries

As well as being on the main pay scale, teachers can boost their careers and incomes by taking on additional responsibilities, such as being a head of year, head of department or subject co-ordinator. These additional responsibilities have a payment attached called a Teaching and Learning Responsibility (TLR) payment. There are two main ranges for TLR payments: TLR 1 and TLR 2. Table 4.2 shows the minimums and maximums of the TLR scales. Where you are on the TLR scale is determined by your school and the type of duties which you undertake.

Table 4.2 TLR payment range (2017)

	TLR1	TLR2
Max	£12,898	£6,450
Min	£7,622	£2,640

Source: https://getintoteaching.education.gov.uk/funding-and-salary/teacher-salaries

There is also a TLR3 payment which can be used for fixed-term projects within schools. This can be for undertaking an additional post such as a co-ordinator for Gifted and Talented or More Able pupils, a Teaching and Learning mentor, a Postgraduate Certificate in Education (PGCE) or NQT mentor, an SMSC or British Values co-ordinator or for any other area which the school deems to be a school improvement priority. For teachers who work with SEN pupils, there is also the possibility of an additional SEN allowance ranging between £2,085–£4,116.

PROGRESSION WITHIN THE SCHOOL ENVIRONMENT

Having looked at the pay scales, we will now turn our attention to possible career progression paths that are available to you once you have established your teaching career. Note that this example is mainly from a secondary viewpoint; however, primary teachers can progress to being deputy heads, computing co-ordinators, CAS Master Teachers, staff governors, and so on.

1. Computer science or computing teacher → Deputy head of computing → Head of computing
2. Computer science or computing teacher → Head of year group
3. Computer science or computing teacher → Head of a key stage

4. Class teacher (primary) → computing co-ordinator
5. Computer science or computing teacher → CAS Hub Leader* → CAS Master Teacher*
6. Computer science or computing teacher → Staff governor*
7. Computer science or computing teacher → Union representative*

   * Job titles marked with an asterix are voluntary.

With the job titles (1–4) described above, the computer science teacher and computing teacher post will fall on the MPS and a TLR would be payable for the other post. The case studies in the next chapter show career progression paths taken by a few such teachers.

Depending on the size of the department, some teachers will find that they skip the post of Deputy Head of Computing and move straight to Head of Computing, either on the first day in post or a few years into post. For teachers who do not wish to follow the academic pathway, there is room within schools to follow a pastoral pathway and combine being a computer science or computing teacher with a head of year group, such as a head of year 7.

There is also the scope for community outreach as part of your role to work as part of the wider computing community and be involved with CAS, such as through being a CAS Hub Leader or a CAS Master Teacher. A CAS Hub Leader hosts events for teachers and likeminded education professionals to meet, share ideas and resources and receive informal training around the computing curriculum. A CAS Master Teacher is a teacher who has upskilled and can support other teachers in the community such as through CAS Hub meetings, with ideas, resources and through running CPD. Both of these roles are beneficial in that they give you support and help to develop your own practice. Another possible role is that of a staff governor. Governors meet with the school's SLT, and other governors such as parent governors, each term to oversee and discuss the strategic leadership of the school, hold the head teacher to account and to keep an eye on the financial management of the school. It is worth noting that CAS Hub Leader, CAS Master Teacher and staff governor roles are unpaid voluntary positions.

For teachers interested in being union representatives there are several teachers' unions. Unions are national organisations, examples of which are the NUT and NASUWT. The purpose of a union is to protect the rights and interests of all teachers. Unions are external to the school and membership is by a fee. Unions can independently advise on profession-related matters such as pay, workload, pensions, health and safety, school policies, flexible working, appraisals and observations, bullying in the workplace, discrimination, maternity matters, safeguarding, termination of employment, redundancy, references and much more. The role of the union representative is to provide the link between the union and teachers and the school's leadership. Union representative roles are also unpaid, but again give a different dimension to a teaching career.

As teachers mature into their careers and move through the pay scales, there are opportunities to undertake qualifications such as the National Professional Qualification in Middle Leadership (NPQML) and the National Professional Qualification in Senior Leadership (NPQSL) for middle and senior leadership roles, although with computing being a shortfall subject you may find yourself in a middle leadership role without having followed the pathway described in this book. If you do find yourself in a middle leadership role through circumstance, it would be a good idea as part of your CPD to undertake middle leadership qualifications, as these support your understanding of recognising outstanding teaching and learning, effective leadership and management strategies, the ability to analyse and interpret performance data, to manage staff, to gain a further understanding of health and safety, safeguarding and much more to support you in gaining further knowledge and confidence.

With senior leadership roles, you are expected to demonstrate leadership through leading and implementing on whole-school improvement priorities by demonstrating skills such as analytical thinking, modelling excellence, holding others to account, self-awareness, working across and with a variety of teams and stakeholders, reviewing the long-term impact of strategies and much more. At NPQSL level, you will have gained skills, confidence and knowledge to lead a highly successful school in the capacity of an assistant or deputy head teacher.

Of course, some of you will aspire to become head teachers. There are also head teacher qualifications by the National Professional Qualification for Headship (NPQH). These would need to be taken after a few years of working as part of a successful leadership team.

PROGRESSION OUTSIDE THE SCHOOL ENVIRONMENT

Let's assume that you have gone as far as you feel possible within a school environment; there are lots of other roles within the education field. Experienced head teachers and SLT staff can also work as OFSTED inspectors; there is potential to become an Education Adviser or Consultant with a variety of organisations, or to become involved in teacher training at colleges or universities. There are lots of options; education is a wide and varied field.

Should you be wondering where you find a teaching job or where you find teachers to recruit, then some suggestions are now offered in Figure 4.2. Good luck in your teaching career!

Figure 4.2 Finding jobs vs recruiting teachers

Places	To find a job	To recruit teachers
School websites	✓	
Direct letter to schools in which you are interested	✓	

(Continued)

155

Figure 4.2 (Continued)

Places	To find a job	To recruit teachers
Through the CAS website (vacancies section)	✓	✓
Links with Initial Teacher Training organisations	✓	✓
Links with BCS Academy	✓	✓
BCS Student Chapters		✓
Offer to train teaching assistants (TAs) – they are already in your school		✓
Graduate teacher internship scheme	✓	✓
TES website	✓	✓
Teaching agencies	✓	✓

5 CASE STUDIES: SNAPSHOTS INTO LIFE IN COMPUTER SCIENCE AND COMPUTING TEACHING

This chapter has been written so that you can 'hear the voice' of serving teachers and their experiences of the computing curriculum. Over these four case studies, there are teachers from non-computing backgrounds and career changers who took different paths into the vocation of teaching, who have differing lengths of service, are primary and secondary teachers, who mention their positives and challenges of the curriculum and of school life. Along with strategies to get the best from pupils and resources used.

CASE STUDY 1: MIXED SECONDARY ACADEMY SCHOOL – SUNBURY-ON-THAMES, SURREY

Number on roll: 907

SEN: 10 students with EHCPs, 18 with statements (same level of support but old and new legislation) which includes 14 in the Communication and Interaction Needs (COIN) Centre and 154 on SEN Support

Jayne Fenton-Hall – Graduate Teacher Programme (GTP) in ICT, BSc (Hons) Information Communication Technology, BCS Certificate in Computer Science Teaching

Career path: From **General Supermarket Assistant** to **Bank Cashier** to **Teacher of ICT** to **Teacher of Computing** to **Gifted and Talented Co-ordinator** to **Head of IT and Computing**

Jayne's career spans over 10 years in secondary schools. Her route into the teacher profession occurred during her late twenties when a change in her personal circumstances meant that she was able to return to education. Driven by a desire for self-improvement, Jayne undertook a degree in IT as she had always had an interest in this area. Upon leaving university, she decided to 'try teaching' as she knew many teachers through friends and family. Jayne applied for a place on a GTP course and completed this at a local secondary school. This led on to a successful job teaching ICT.

As the news of the changes to the computing curriculum came into being, Jayne was in a new school with a head of department who was a CAS Master Teacher, who was very enthusiastic about the new curriculum and ran the local CAS Hub. The school implemented the new curriculum one year earlier than required nationally and this time was used to iron out any issues and to find out areas for development within the new curriculum. This meant attending CAS Hub meetings and upskilling through courses. The first step on the upskilling path was to attend a Python programming course offered through Queen Mary University. The course focused on computing theory and programming which gave Jayne an excellent understanding of programming concepts.

Jayne has found many positives in the new curriculum:

- At key stage 3, pupils have lots of opportunities to explore through kinaesthetic activity.

- At a teacher level, the growth in her own knowledge meant that she gained a greater appreciation for the digital world.

- At a pupil level, the curriculum broadened the scope for pupils. Currently in her school some pupils at key stage 4 have chosen to study ICT and computer science qualifications as they can appreciate the 'whole industry'.

Some of the early challenges of implementing the curriculum she found were:

- Writing schemes of work and ensuring a smooth progression through key stage 3.

- Depth of knowledge required within the new specification at GCSE level and finding the time to upskill.

- Funding for new resources to support the curriculum, such as textbooks and equipment for physical computing such as Raspberry Pis, Pico Boards, Makey Makey boards, and so on, as buying in class sets can be quite expensive for classes of 30 when managing on a limited budget.

Some of the best resources that Jayne uses to assist in delivery of the curriculum are:

For all the curriculum

- www.teach-ict.com
- Axsied Resources – https://www.axsied.com/
- BBC Bitesize – www.bbc.co.uk/education
- https://www.cambridgegcsecomputing.org/

For teaching of Python skills

- http://pynewbs.com/

At Jayne's school, pupils at key stage 3 benefit from one hour of computing time per week and at key stage 4, pupils have six hours a fortnight. Pupils have a greater amount of time at key stage 4 due to the rigour of the new specifications and preparation required for examinable components, given the high number of SEN within the school. The offerings for GCSE level are either a computer science qualification – OCR GCSE Computer Science or the OCR Cambridge Nationals iMedia, which appeals to pupils who wish to pursue an ICT type route. The reasons behind the choice of awarding body here are an engaging and well-structured specification – which is easy for a teacher to deliver and clear to a pupil in terms of weightings and requirements, available resources and forums on social media with subject experts who respond quickly to questions.

Jayne has found that cross-curricular links and STEM enrichment have been key in assisting pupils to appreciate the subject. For example, collaboration with the maths department in the early stages of teaching 'Number Systems' assisted her with an understanding of how students are taught place value for denary numbers. She also discussed terminology with science and technology to ensure correct use, focusing mainly around circuits (current, flow, and so on) as well as discussing when in the Scheme of Work[81] they use transistors and when they cover logic gates. Jayne was then able to apply common strategies and terminology in computing lessons.

Through STEM activities the computing department has enjoyed events such as an RAF roadshow aimed at years 8 and 9, where pupils learnt about how STEM was covered in the RAF. Pupils learnt about how virtual reality (VR) is used such as in flight simulations for pilots and the RAF also demonstrated a drone (flying it in front of the students). They discussed cybersecurity and how drones can be intercepted, giving a further demonstration which involved flying the drone and letting another facilitator intercept it. Pupils also benefitted from a 'Heathrow Coding Challenge' workshop, where pupils built a robot from Lego Mindstorms, learnt how to program the robot and then practised controlling the robot. Pupils are encouraged to enter competitions such as the BAFTA Young Games Designer competition, which allows pupils to explore different areas of making a video game. Through these activities pupils can appreciate practical applications of computer science outside the classroom.

As part of her upskilling journey, Jayne also completed the BCS Certificate in Computer Science Teaching, as this provided a means to have a recognised qualification for teaching the curriculum. This involved documenting 20 hours of CPD, which was achieved through attendance of CAS Hubs and focusing on learning Linux for teaching the GCSE and an essay on pedagogy (which explored the approach of paired programming and a programming project in Python). For the programming project, Jayne designed and successfully developed a Python programming project with a Graphical

User Interface (GUI), to ensure that she had the required knowledge and skills to teach this area.

Another part of her professional journey came when the head of department left the school; at this stage Jayne took over the running of the CAS Hub, as when she was an attendee, she had found it an excellent forum for information and networking. She continues to run a successful hub and undertook CAS Master Teacher training for self-knowledge, to support her department and wider colleagues.

During a part of her career, Jayne has also held a whole-school responsibility of 'Gifted and Talented Co-ordinator'. This has made Jayne aware of the need for diversity and inclusion methods that reach all within the classroom.

Some of the teaching methods employed within Jayne's department are:

- Scaffolding – such as when coding, through giving partial code and getting pupils to work to develop the code.
- Modelling – showing pupils possible approaches to a solution.
- Other media to support learning – videos, websites.
- Stretch activities – extension activities for the more able, which are not just more work but where independent working (individual, paired or group) is encouraged and the challenge is greater. For example, when coding, pupils learn how to make a text-based menu, but can explore how to make a GUI, through using the Python GUI tool Tkinter.
- One-to-one support through TAs.
- Catch-up sessions at lunchtime, afterschool and focused revision sessions.
- For areas such as raising the number of girls taking up the subject, across school, national days celebrating females and women in STEM are held such as

'International Women's Day' and 'Ada Lovelace Day'. Currently less than 1 per cent of girls opted to study computer science at key stage 4 while 7 per cent of girls opted to study ICT at key stage 4.

- Homework booklets at key stage 3, so that homework is accessible to all pupils, regardless of computer access. The booklets contain the resources, questions and answer spaces. This also supports pupils in developing written answers as they progress along their schooling journey to GCSE which requires in-depth writing. Questions in the booklets are differentiated and range from 'State, Give, Explain', 'Describe and Discuss' style questions. An example of a 'Discuss' style question is: *Discuss the following statement covering all points of view: People who need accessible websites should pay something towards the extra costs of development.*

- SMSC booklets: the school has SMSC as a priority on their development plan and pupils have SMSC booklets in which they are encouraged to give opinions, on areas such as AI, online friends versus real friends, the digital divide, and so on. An example of a question from the SMSC booklet is: *Online and console games have Pan European Game Information (PEGI) age ratings to stop children playing inappropriate games. Do you think age ratings should be used for online and console games? Give reasons for and against.*

- To manage areas such as coding, which many can find challenging, across the department the approach taken is to underpin underlying concepts such as Sequence, Selection, Iteration, Inputs, Variables, Outputs, and so on, with unplugged activities. This is then followed by delivering programming concepts individually before getting pupils to attempt writing long programs. For example, pupils will explore short programs for getting an input from a user, using an IF statement, different types of loop and how they function, file handling, string manipulation, and so on. Examples are now provided.

http://pynewbs.com/1a/creating-variables/

↓ **Practice Task 2**

1. Write a variable with the name FirstName and the value as your first name.

2. Write a variable with the name Surname and the value as your surname.

3. Print the FirstName variable. (Use the variable name FirstName, not just your first name in speech marks)

4. Print the Surname variable.

http://pynewbs.com/6a/a/

↓ **Practice Task 3**

1. Ask the user to input a number. Print "Are we there yet?" that number of times.

2. Ask the user their name and their age. Print their name the number of times as their age.

Once pupils have explored each of these, they are then set 'coding challenges' that require multiple skills. Before attempting the challenge, the pupils undertake a paired or group activity and annotate the challenge with the skills that would be required to reach a solution. With this understanding fully cemented, pupils can either code in the department's language of choice – Python – or they are free to work independently and look up what an IF statement looks like in another language, thus extending their skill and understanding. Unplugged activities are also used throughout key stage 3 and if required at key stage 4, for topics such as searching and sorting, algorithms and number systems.

Across school and within her department, Jayne has found that one of the big areas in which pupils need ongoing education is safeguarding. The department and the wider school achieve this through:

- celebration of Safer Internet Day events;
- assemblies;

- online safety topics included in the homework booklets;
- outside speakers;
- the curriculum;
- participation in National Anti-Bullying Week events;
- recognition of National Cyber Security Awareness month.

The school also makes use of internet security software, of which Securus is an example, web filtering software such as Smoothwall and classroom management software such as Netsupport. Using a range of monitoring tools keeps pupils safe. In the event of a pupil using the school systems inappropriately, this is managed by the classroom teacher, the safeguarding team and SLT depending upon severity.

In addition to subject knowledge, some of the skills employed by Jayne both in her role as teacher and head of department are:

- organisation and planning – of lessons, teacher and departmental duties;
- behaviour management;
- motivation and persuasion – getting pupils to make the right choices in the classroom and to be enthusiastic about the subject;
- observation – being able to see what is going on everywhere in the classroom and being aware of what pupils are doing at all times;
- analysing and assessing – such as deciding the best fit when grading GCSE work, analysing class and departmental data;
- decision making – such as deciding to exclude a pupil from lesson, the qualifications to deliver at key stage 4, the STEM and enrichment activities to be offered;
- communication and presentation – this covers good interaction with pupils, parents and immediate colleagues, senior leadership, governors and many more.

Within the classroom, some of the feedback and assessment strategies in place are verbal feedback, written feedback in books, self and peer assessment, AfL techniques such as traffic light cards to check understanding and mini white boards for quick capture of understanding.

In terms of behaviour management, an area of conflict can occur in the IT classroom with pupils leaving their seats to access printouts at the printer. In Jayne's classroom, this is simply not allowed. She collects the printouts and either distributes them herself or checks the work and then returns work to pupils. Jayne's advice for any teacher struggling with behaviour management is to follow departmental and school policy, be consistent and fair, reward the positive whenever you can and always follow everything through.

REFLECTION POINTS FROM THIS CASE STUDY

- Non-teaching experience – career route.
- BCS Computer Science Teaching certificate.
- CAS Hub Leader.
- CAS Master Teacher.
- Other whole-school experience.
- Safeguarding.
- Homework booklets.
- SMSC booklets.
- Pedagogy – unplugged, paired, group activity.
- EHCP (SEN).
- Resources.
- STEM activity.
- Behaviour management.

CASE STUDY 2: MIXED SECONDARY ACADEMY SCHOOL – LEATHERHEAD, SURREY

Number on roll: 750

Steve Clarke – PGCE Business Studies, BA (Hons) Business Studies

Career path: From **Teaching Assistant** to **Business and ICT teacher** to **ICT teacher** to **Education consultant** to **Director of Computing and Curriculum consultant**. Additionally, a **Parent Governor** at a primary school.

Steve's journey into education and computing started off after completing a business degree at university. The degree had a one-year industry placement and during this year Steve worked in marketing. After university, Steve returned to the marketing company for six months. Steve then took six months travelling. On his return, he worked for PC World[82] in marketing. This is where the IT and computing link began. Steve realised that an office job was not what he wanted; he did however feel a passion for education, which was encouraged and supported by his wife who was training to be a teacher. Steve took a TA position to get a feel for the job. He thoroughly enjoyed the work and gained a good understanding of differentiation and inclusion. This led onto taking a PGCE course.

The placement during the PGCE was an 11–18 placement which was 50–50 business and ICT. The ICT side was a challenge but enjoyable, due to having very supportive colleagues. Steve took over leadership of the department in his second year and held this role for a further seven years, which also included a stint as head of faculty for design technology and secondment to the senior leadership team, during which time he led several whole-school ICT projects. This was then followed by a change in career direction and a few years as an education consultant. He has now returned to the teaching profession.

At Steve's school the national curriculum is studied by all pupils in key stage 3. Pupils get one hour of computing time a fortnight. At key stage 4, pupils are following the Edexcel Computer Science specification and are timetabled for five hours per fortnight. At key stage 3 the coding language(s) used are Scratch, Micro:bit Microsoft Block Editor, Micro-python and Python. The coding language used at GCSE is Python. At A-level there are plans to follow a BTEC in computing, to allow for a blend of ICT and computer science. The reasons behind this are due to cohort size and the needs of the learners. Classes across the board are small as the school only has roughly 750 pupils across three key stages.

The main challenges that Steve faced when taking this post was a lack of staff. The school had previously struggled with recruiting ICT and computing teachers, hence the small amount of allocated lesson time at key stage 3. In taking this role, a new department was being created. The next challenge faced was getting all pupils to a basic level of 'Digital Literacy' before teaching computer science. This included teaching pupils housekeeping tasks such as good folder structure, naming of files and how to save files. Once this had been done, Steve then started teaching the computer science concepts through the use of unplugged activities. It is interesting to note here that a ready-made Scheme of Work and resources would not have worked in this situation due to the needs of the pupils. The requirement here was for Steve to be adaptable.

Another challenge was to find resources that did not always have a mathematical element, as this can be off-putting to some pupils who are already struggling with maths. To this end, where maths has been unavoidable, such as when teaching binary, it has to be made interesting. Steve achieved this through unplugged activities and also a bit of music in the background, to which the pupils made a little dance and made the lesson fun. The same principles were applied when teaching topics such as two's complement notation.

For Steve, the difference between the old curriculum and this new one is that the previous curriculum was easier to learn and easier to find a teacher from any discipline who could teach 'some presentation skills', whereas it is challenging to find a teacher to do even a small amount of Python coding. In Steve's opinion, the problem for a non-computer science specialist is that it takes quite a bit of time to learn the theory required to deliver a successful and impactful one-hour lesson, alongside making the lesson interesting and differentiating for pupils.

While there have been challenges, Steve has embraced and found many positives in the new curriculum, as he recognises that the subject known as ICT had in some cases been devalued through lack of rigour. Through the new curriculum, the profile of computing and computer science has been raised and emphasis placed on its relevance in today's world and our futures.

When planning a lesson, some of the best resources that Steve utilises are:

- Craig 'n' Dave resources – for A-level and GCSE, which he uses for Flipped Learning.
- CAS resources.
- 'Challenge Chips' – this was inspired by a display which was shared on Twitter (source unknown) to build in challenge for all topics that are taught. Pupils are able to choose a 'challenge chip' (that is, a laminated card) and to stretch themselves through the activities on the challenge chip. Examples are shown in Appendix 7.
- Coding challenges and projects available at www.101computing.net/ and https://inventwithpython. com/

In planning a lesson Steve goes through the following process:

i.   checks the CAS website to see what has already been done;
ii. seeks unplugged ways of teaching the topic;
iii. does a general internet search on the topic.

Having a background in business and ICT, a good question to ask is how did Steve gain his computing knowledge? This was achieved through self-teaching, online tutorials and also through being an education consultant, where he was tasked with seeking out the best way to support the curriculum. Steve has taught for nine years and was also an education consultant for three years, managing schools through the transition to computing. It is a business approach to the curriculum that has contributed to his success.

From his early days as a TA, when Steve became passionate about supporting disadvantaged pupils, he noted a statement that you may well hear in teaching: 'Computer science is not for weaker ability pupils'. Steve has spent considerable amounts of time proving this statement wrong, as the curriculum is for everyone. Within his own practice, his approach is **'the teacher is the TA'**. Starting with a well-planned lesson, Steve introduces the topic and pupils then commence working; his first focus is to then check on the 'disadvantaged' pupils within the group and do one-to-one or small group work with them if required. This then asks the question, how are the needs of the more-able pupils met? To this end, Steve has embedded 'challenge chips' into all of his lessons, so that pupils do not sit waiting for the next task, but are independent learners who are able to go to the 'challenge chip' box and to select a task, which stretches that pupil.

Another way in which Steve provides an inclusive classroom is through the use of 'Collaboration Cards'. Initially this requires quite a bit of planning, but once implemented, works well. The concept here is that each child has their own card in their book which is colour coded, has different icons and names such as Hexadecimal, ASCII, the name of a programming language, the name of an operating system, and so on. In this way, Steve is then able to say 'work in your ASCII group' or 'work in your Hexadecimal group'. Due to the pre-planning, groups can then end up being mixed ability, supportive abilities, challenging abilities, pupils that work well together, and so on. This allows for a very fluid classroom and also supports behaviour management, as Steve is not at any point saying Sarah work with John, or Sarah work with Joanne, for example, which can lead to pupils saying 'I don't like him or her'.

Further techniques used are to challenge pupils to think and discuss articles in the news to highlight the relevance of computer science and to bring SMSC into lessons in an interesting way. For example, a standout lesson was pondering an article featuring 'Elon Musk'[83] on links between AI and bio-engineering, generating class discussion around points such as 'are we just a computer simulation?'[84] This was such an exciting point one disadvantaged student continued the discussion at home with his family and has since been inspired to work harder in computer science. The point of these discussions is for wonder, amazement and to ignite the imagination of perhaps the next inventor, or simply for a pupil to interact and question their environment in a different way. All food for thought.

REFLECTION POINTS FROM THIS CASE STUDY

- Non-teaching experience – career route.
- TA experience.
- 11–18 experience.
- Strategies to be used when pupils have poor IT skills.
- Not using a ready-made Scheme of Work.
- Pedagogy – unplugged activities.
- Differentiation techniques and activity (see Appendix 7).
- Challenge Chips and Collaboration Cards (see Appendix 7).
- Resources.
- SMSC.

CASE STUDY 3: MIXED PRIMARY SCHOOL (STATE) – CHERTSEY, SURREY

Number on roll: 210–250 (one form entry) – 51 per cent SEN

Kathie Drake – PGCE Primary Education, BSc (Hons) Business Information Systems

Career path: From a career in **Industry** to **Learning Support Assistant** to **Year 2 teacher or Computing Subject Co-ordinator**

Kathie's computing journey started off with a degree in Business Information Systems. This was then followed by a 10-year career in industry working with Oracle databases. In her personal life, she was also a qualified fitness instructor. When Kathie became a mother she then did a series of part-time jobs which included being a Learning Support Assistant (LSA) at both primary and secondary schools. Realising how much she enjoyed training people, through fitness instructing, and the satisfaction she felt as an LSA working with children, she felt the need to contribute towards shaping and moulding tomorrow's citizens. This led to undertaking a primary PGCE; she is now two years into her teaching career.

As a primary teacher, Kathie teaches all subjects on the National Curriculum including computing. This is the case for all teachers within the school. However, with her computing background, Kathie has also been given the role of computing subject co-ordinator across the school. Having had no prior experience of the old curriculum, Kathie was able to approach computing with a 'fresh slate'. In Kathie's school, each year group benefits from a dedicated 50 minutes per week for the computing curriculum. IT Support[85] is bought in half a day per week for general IT support. However, the school has not bought a computing Scheme of Work.

In fulfilling her role as computing subject co-ordinator and supporting the school's other teachers in covering the computing curriculum, Kathie has found the curriculum to be open, allowing for great flexibility in approach. An unfortunate side-effect of this is that different training providers can and have offered various interpretations around terminology, digital literacy and other parts of the curriculum. Without a dedicated provider or Scheme of Work, staff are left with an unclear picture of what constitutes coverage of the curriculum and with varied understanding of the terminology within it. That aside, it has been possible for Kathie to pull together a Scheme of Work from various non-paid for resources for the school's teachers to use, as well as give guidance on their use. Kathie feels that the next step is to develop staff knowledge of CT and cross-curricular computing. One possible future strategy she has is for staff to undergo training with Barefoot Computing, to gain insight into building unplugged activities and terminology into lessons across the curriculum.

The current Scheme of Work addresses computer science and CT in key stage 1 with the use of Beebots. For key stage 2, pupils use Scratch software to also develop coding skills. Computing subject time, for all pupils, is also used to cover and reinforce eSafety. Kathie urged the use of wider computing skills within this activity, such that key stage 1 pupils get to make posters on which they use images that they find online. Similarly, key stage 2 pupils make PowerPoint presentations on the subject which they present to their peers and parents during school assembly.

A future aspiration that Kathie has is for all classes to keep a blog, thus giving pupils access to using digital equipment and producing digital material. It is her belief that the blog would give the pupils a sense of ownership and of audience, similarly to the use of PowerPoint presentations. This approach would be cross-curricular allowing for the use of photography and video whilst focusing on topics that the classes cover in other subject areas. This would allow pupils further opportunities to gain and strengthen presenting skills.

A particular challenge that Kathie highlights is the high level of SEN within the school. With many pupils still learning to read and write, there is a fair amount of intervention work taking place, as required, and also one-to-one sessions for pupils who fall behind with maths and English. Within this context, she is mindful that basic keyboard skills cannot be taken for granted as pupils may not recognise all upper and lower case letters, or numerals, let alone know special characters. Consequently, emphasis is also placed upon the understanding of the keyboard before using the computer. This is one way in which unplugged activities are highly beneficial within the primary environment. Kathie goes on to note that one way of tackling resourcing issues, such as not having enough Beebots, is to use FakeBots[86] as an effective alternate resource.

Through pupil and some parental enquiry at the school, there has been interest in coding enrichment activities. Kathie runs a code club across key stage 2, where pupils can further develop coding skills in Scratch. There are also plans to introduce pupils to the basics of text-based programming in the coding club. There is a good balance between girls and boys within the club and Kathie believes that the club is an excellent place for pupils to explore, review and evaluate concepts through paired and group activities.

In terms of general teaching, Kathie has not encountered any particular behavioural problems in the classroom. As with any other environment, there are cases where pupils are unkind to each other. However, the focus on eSafety is an effective preventative strategy for safeguarding against online bullying. Kathie also stresses that the school has a strong emphasis on getting the pupils to understand the consequences of their actions, as a policy across the board.

Being computing subject co-ordinator, Kathie has found that all and any IT-related issues can come to her. With the budget constraints that all schools have, dedicated IT support for staff and infrastructure is limited. When the paid-for support is unavailable, Kathie is the de facto go-to person, irrespective of whether it is in support of the computing curriculum or not.

Kathie summarises teaching in general as follows:

> the actual teaching part of the job is very enjoyable, it is the additional paperwork and administration tasks that are time consuming.

REFLECTION POINTS FROM THIS CASE STUDY

- Non-teaching experience – career route.
- LSA experience.
- Behaviour built into school ethos.
- Pedagogy – unplugged activities.
- High numbers of SEN pupils.
- Intervention work.
- Enrichment activities.
- Safeguarding/eSafety.
- Future plans to train staff.
- Not using a ready-made Scheme of Work.
- Managing resourcing issues.

CASE STUDY 4: MIXED SECONDARY COMMUNITY SCHOOL – PICKERING, NORTH YORKSHIRE

Number on roll: 890

SEN: Enhanced Mainstream School (EMS), Dyslexia Quality Mark

Chris Sharples – PGCE Science, BSc (Hons) Physics

Career path: From **Science teacher** to **York Local Education Authority (LEA) (curriculum support)** to **Head of ICT** to **Computing Teacher** to **Head of Computing or CAS Master Teacher** and **Hub Leader**

Like many computing teachers, Chris has grown up in a rapidly evolving digital age. He started learning BBC Basic for the first ever computer studies O-level, using BBC Master computers, and still retains wonder at writing code to sort strings alphabetically.

When Chris decided to enter the teaching profession many advised him against this decision. However, a head teacher friend explained the positives of being in the profession and making a difference. This was in 1989. Chris undertook a PGCE and became a science teacher. He was always looking for ways to enhance teaching and learning and this evolved with the use of ICT including data logging using old PCs in his laboratory. This was a pain because then other science teachers would book his room and he would have to move out. This was solved by creating a PC suite specifically for the science department. It was this work that enabled him to be an associate with the Science Consortium for New Opportunities Fund (NOF) training when he went on to work for York LEA in the Project 'Schools Learning Together' funded by the Gatsby Charitable Foundation. His main role was helping to develop a bespoke website and then a VLE to support York Schools teachers and students.

As ICT came on stream, Chris wanted to continue to use ICT, and gained a post as head of ICT at his current school, Lady Lumley's School in Pickering, North Yorkshire. It was a steep learning curve, but with the help of an able colleague, the department was judged exemplary within three years by Her Majesty's Inspectors (OFSTED HMI). The curriculum consisted of a creative digital course – Edexcel's level 2 CiDA, and the Applied ICT A-level. The creative aspects and teamwork approach encouraged girls to make up more than half of the 60 or so key stage 4 students and subsequent 12 or so key stage 5 students each year. Chris also developed student 'Digital Leaders' to help develop a shared aim of **'Competent and confident teachers and students focused on purposeful learning through using technology'**.

Move forward 10 years, and as the new computing curriculum came into effect, it presented and still presents a challenge for many ICT teachers not having a computing background. However, refusing to 'give over to the dark side', Chris upskilled and attended the York Picademy course to become a Raspberry Pi certified educator. Re-imagining a classroom of BBC Master computers, Chris and his Digital Leaders then set up a class set of Raspberry Pis. Chris has become a CAS Master Teacher and is just organising the first Ryedale Hub Meeting for primary schools in the area. He sees links with primary feeders to be very important, as well as the opportunity to bring in the expertise of secondary CAS Master Teachers in the region to support primary colleagues.

Lady Lumley's School is a mixed comprehensive and the lessons are 1 hour 40 minutes long, making three lessons in the school day. At key stage 3 the conversion to a computing curriculum is now complete with the introduction of the last year 9 unit – using Micropython on BBC Micro:bits. The programming languages used are Scratch in year 7 for visual programming and Python in years 8 and 9 for text-based programming. All the units are designed to provide challenge and engagement, as well as giving year 9s the opportunity to gauge their potential for choosing and thence being successful with computer science at key stage 4. At GCSE, students follow the Eduqas awarding body specifications which will then follow through onto A-level Eduqas.

Within the classroom, the biggest challenges faced have been:

- Going from teaching ICT which is very practical to teaching computer science or computing which has a large theory and examinable component. This has meant learning techniques on how to better answer exam-style questions and assist students in learning large amounts of theory.

- Learning the pedagogy of teaching computer science.

- Fitting activities together so that the curriculum is coherent and gets progressively challenging.

- Gaining subject knowledge and getting a good understanding of computer science.

- Having to explain to parents that the curriculum is new and their child has not gained all of the necessary knowledge at key stage 3 (because the subject is new), so that there is an extra workload at key stage 4. Although this is improving year on year as the curriculum is embedded at key stage 3.

- The increased intensity of supporting students with coding which is much more mentally challenging than learning the skills required for ICT qualifications.

While there have been challenges, there is a wealth of resources which have supported the transition, starting with #caschat (on Twitter) and Facebook groups. Chris has used many resources from the CAS website, as well as books and other websites. The best book has been a first-year computer science university text (see Brookshear and Brylow, 2014) as it gives the overall 'big' picture, as well as being based on Python. Chris also collates 'best resources' on his personal website to share with teachers (see 'Additional references').

In terms of diversity in the classroom, there has been a need to focus on girls in getting them to take up computer science, as this year's (2016–17) cohort has five female students out of 22. However, Chris quickly realised that positive discrimination in the classroom has its own drawbacks and as such works on the principles of 'good computer science for all', as many of the techniques used for girls were equally applicable to boys and students of differing abilities. Chris offers the following example from his experiences.

A female student had a meltdown over coding and through talks with the student and parent, Chris suggested watching Reshma Saujani's YouTube video 'Teach girls bravery not perfection'. This TED Talk explores girls being brave enough to take chances, as they do not like to be seen making mistakes or being a failure. This comes back to the Challenge for all theme, but also building resilience. The girl involved now quotes that she 'is getting there' which is a great open mindset phrase.

Chris has found that part of the success in delivering the curriculum well has been down to good infrastructure. This translates into all students having access to resources online, via the school VLE and 'Google Apps for Education'.

Additionally, he expects a lot from students both in and out of the classroom. For example, during the summer holidays, Chris set homework via 'Codecademy or Khan Academy' so that students could improve their coding skills. This was a useful platform as it also allows a teacher to track student progress through the various modules. Additionally, success comes from being aware of the student's previous experiences at primary school as well as an appropriate baseline test.

Some of the top methods employed in Chris's classroom to get the best out of the students are:

- paired programming;
- use of mini white boards to capture quick responses and include all students;
- effective questioning to develop logic reasoning skills;
- flipped learning for theoretical concepts;
- modelling exam answers;
- mind mapping theory units;
- flash cards for revision;
- peer support.

Underlying this is having excellent organisation, clear explanations and high expectations.

Chris believes that it is his job to inspire confidence in his students (and colleagues) so that they have the grit and determination to overcome the significant challenges that come with the computing curriculum. His Digital Leaders mantra still applies – 'Competent and confident teachers and students focused on purposeful learning through using technology'.

REFLECTION POINTS FROM THIS CASE STUDY

- Non-teaching experience – career route.
- Science background.
- Digital Leaders.
- 11–18 experience.
- CAS Master Teacher.
- CAS Hub Leader.
- Links with primary feeder schools.
- Diversity with girls.
- VLE and out of school learning.
- Resources.
- Pedagogy.
- SEN/Enhanced Mainstream School.
- Raspberry Pi Certified Educator.

6 CONCLUSION

Hopefully, by now you have a clear overview of what life is like in the classroom for a computer science teacher and in school generally. Before we conclude this journey into the computing classroom and school life, there are a few suggestions and points to ponder and reflect on.

It would be a good idea to start learning a few computer science concepts if you haven't already, then learn a few unplugged activities to explain these concepts, followed by learning to program in a text-based programming language such as Python. You could then attempt to build your own website or program an electronic board as part of a fun physical computing exercise. Think about how you would explain what you have done to an audience, think about ways of engaging an audience in the activity. All the guidelines for teaching have not yet been invented and you may stumble across a unique method for differentiation.

Having thought of and practised a few activities for the computing classroom, let us turn our attention to teaching captions in the media. Frequently in the press there are headlines such as 'teachers have lots of holidays – they shouldn't complain about workload', 'teachers leaving the profession due to workload', 'teacher burnout is at an all-time high', 'lack of funding', 'teacher shortages'. These can be off-putting headlines and make you wonder – how does one stay committed to the profession in the face of such headlines?

It is certainly true that education has experienced many changes recently and some of these have increased workload.

However, the curriculum has been introduced, specifications have been updated and, for the most part, we are now settling.

As with all education systems, there will be qualifications taken away or added at differing levels such as the new T-levels; however, subject knowledge is what we are focused on and dealing with pupils, so new qualifications should not adversely affect your practice. The Digital Age and computing specialist teachers are here to stay. The best advice is that teaching is a multifaceted job, which can become demanding; the trick is to pace yourself and be very organised. Allocate set times for tasks such as marking and report writing. When you have your holidays, ensure that they are exactly that: your holidays, not time to be spent marking or planning (this can be tricky to do).

Remember the reason that you have holidays is for you to relax. In many other jobs people work set hours and do a set task, or have the flexibility of being able to take a day off to undertake a personal activity; however, this is not the case for teaching. This is not a profession which offers nine-to-five hours; teachers do not have the 'luxury' of having an 'off day'. Once a teacher sets foot on a school's premises, they are in demand; many times pupils will greet you at the door, asking questions and statements that can range from – 'What are we doing today?', 'Do I have a lesson with you today?', 'Miss or Sir, I have forgotten my book, I have forgotten my homework, I don't have my book!'. This may all happen before you even get to the staffroom or your office. Then there may be further matters to attend to such as returning a phone call to a parent or an email to a parent or another colleague; this is all before the teaching day commences. Teachers are always 'ON'.

Enjoy your career, you are a subject specialist and are in short supply, you are also an important part of a great machine; the link between child, parent, school, community and the wider world.

Think back to your grandparents' generation, compare what technology they had and what you now take for granted (this is a frequent activity used in schools, however, sometimes the pupils do not appreciate the changes). For some of us the differences can be great, such as TV, colour tv, digital tv, digital radio, email, the internet, online banking, online ordering, chip and pin cards, virtual reality, smartphones, the supermarket, wagon to car, to cars with on-board computers to self-driving cars. There are multiple devices in every house with information at our fingertips and emerging possibilities with digital currencies such as Bitcoins. In short, everything has changed. Consider what three or four generations on from you may possibly take for granted. This is quite mind-boggling. If in any doubt as to the purpose you are serving and you're perhaps thinking, can society and humankind advance any further, consider the following quote, which sums up perfectly why the job of the computer science teacher is relevant.

> When I was 16 I learnt to touch type. I knew I wasn't going to be a secretary, but it was a skill for the future. This is exactly the same concept being applied to computer science and computational thinking.
>
> Kathie Drake
> Primary Computing Co-ordinator and Year 2 teacher

In short, as a computer science and computing specialist you are permanently standing on the edge of change and somewhere within the UK is a teacher who is currently teaching a pupil who is capable of making great advancements for society through the use of digital technologies. That teacher could, at some point in your career, be you.

APPENDIX 1
SELF-ASSESSMENTS

Use the grids in this appendix, in conjunction with the attributes, knowledge and skills section in Chapter 2; you can self-assess your strengths and areas for development.

Attribute Self-Assessment – **place a tick ✓ in the relevant box or a few words of inspiration**

Attribute	Requires development?	Developed?	How can I develop this area?
Organisation and preparation			
Reflection			
Listening			
Empathy			
Curiosity			
Respectful			
Authoritative			
Cross-curricular thinker			
Good communicator			
Approachable			

Knowledge Self-Assessment – **place a tick ✓ in the relevant box or a few words of inspiration**

Knowledge	Requires development?	Developed?	How can I develop this area?
Working knowledge of the curriculum or programme of study or pedagogy of computer science			
Working knowledge of at least one awarding body at key stages 4 and 5 (secondary only)			
Understanding of prior key stages			
Understanding of onward key stages			
Diversity within computing			
Working knowledge of the teachers' standards			

(Continued)

Knowledge	Requires development?	Developed?	How can I develop this area?
Working knowledge of the BCS Certificate in Computer Science Teaching			
Technical skills			
The school values and vision			
How the school fits in the community			
Understanding of other subjects and departments			
Understanding of local and national initiatives for the subject and for education in general			

Skills Self-Assessment – **place a tick ✓ in the relevant box or a few words of inspiration**

Subject-specific skills	Requires development?	Developed?	How can I develop this area?
Abstraction			
Algorithmic design			
Decomposition			
Pattern recognition			
Generalisation			
Evaluation			
General skills			
Leadership			
Problem solver			
Ability to maintain good relationships with other staff, pupils and parents			
Enthuse, inspire, influence			
Celebrate achievement			
Budget management			
Advise			

(Continued)

Subject-specific skills	Requires development?	Developed?	How can I develop this area?
Adaptability			
Patience			
Behaviour management			
Delegation			

APPENDIX 2
SEATING PLAN

Class: _____ **Seating Plan**

Pupil / Desk7		Desk8 / Pupil	Desk9 / Pupil	Desk10 / Pupil	Desk11 / Pupil
Pupil / Desk6					Desk12 / Pupil
Pupil / Desk5					Desk13 / Pupil
Pupil / Desk4					Desk14 / Pupil
Pupil / Desk3		Pupil / Desk33	Pupil / Desk28		Desk15 / Pupil
Pupil / Desk2		Pupil / Desk32	Pupil / Desk27		Desk16 / Pupil
Pupil / Desk1		Pupil / Desk31	Pupil / Desk26		Desk17 / Pupil
		Pupil / Desk30	Pupil / Desk25		Desk18 / Pupil
Door		Pupil / Desk29			Desk19 / Pupil
					Desk20 / Pupil
			Teacher		Desk21 / Pupil
Workbench			Smart Board	Printer	Desk22 / Pupil
					Desk23 / Pupil
					Desk24

APPENDIX 3
JOB ADVERTS

In this Appendix, the full job adverts referenced in Chapter 2 are included.

SUNBURY MANOR SCHOOL JOB APPLICATION PACK

The complete job application pack for the role of teacher of computing and IT at Sunbury Manor School is detailed below.

Sunbury Manor School – Full letter from head teacher

Dear Applicant,

Thank you for the interest you have shown in Sunbury Manor, described by a recent visiting parent as having **'joy coming from every corner'**. We are extremely proud to be a happy and highly inclusive school.

Our students are our greatest assets and we are very proud that our school is, as another visiting parent described, **'welcoming and nurturing whilst stretching, providing a learning ethic of a very high standard'**. We have to be the source of security, support and challenge for so many of our students and the calm, work-focused, good humoured environment for which we strive at all times is a safe haven for so many. We provide outstanding care to our students, by understanding and working to remove the barriers to education which affect so many, enabling them to attend, achieve, be happy and succeed. We prepare them for the next step and beyond, by raising aspirations for them and their families, providing relentless support and the challenge to achieve the best results of which they are capable.

Sunbury Manor School began the new academic year with the best GCSE results the school has ever seen and we are now placed in the top 25 per cent of similar schools nationally.

In March 2016, we had an Ofsted inspection and I am delighted to share some of the key highlights below. The full letter can be viewed on the school website www.sunburymanor.surrey.sch. uk and it confirms that the school continues to be good and that the good quality of education has been maintained since the last inspection. We were delighted that they stated that;

This is a very inclusive school that serves its community well.

The school is a safe, happy and harmonious environment.

You and other leaders have developed an aspirational culture where the main focus is on the quality of teaching and learning. Consequently, teaching remains good.

Behaviour around the school is good, with calm and orderly movement between classes and at break times. Pupils are respectful of their environment with very little litter or damage seen in the buildings. Pupils are polite and helpful to visitors, holding doors open for them. Pupils wear their uniform smartly and are proud of their school.

I am so proud of our students, staff and governors and so pleased that their hard work and dedication has been recognised. We are united as a school and face all challenges with determination and relentless positivity and were delighted by a recent parent comment that we are **'a school that is concerned with the whole well-being of their children, rather than just being a results factory'**.

This is a very exciting time for our school and I look forward to receiving an application from you and welcoming you to the school in the near future.

With best wishes,

Louise Duncan

Sunbury Manor School – Full job description

RESPONSIBLE TO

- Head of Department

OVERALL RESPONSIBILITY

- To plan and develop high quality lessons and courses, using a variety of approaches, to continually enhance teaching and learning.
- To maintain and build upon the teaching standards achieved in the award for QTS (Secondary) as set out by the Secretary of State.

SECTION 1 – GENERAL TEACHING DUTIES

Teaching and Learning

1. Manage pupil learning through effective teaching in accordance with the Department's schemes of work and policies.
2. Ensure continuity, progression and cohesiveness in all teaching.
3. Use a variety of methods and approaches (including differentiation) to match curricular objectives and the range of pupil needs, and ensure equal opportunity for all pupils.
4. Set homework regularly (in accordance with the School homework policy), to consolidate and extend learning and encourage pupils to take responsibility for their own learning.
5. Work with SEN staff and support staff (including prior discussion and joint planning) in order to benefit from their specialist knowledge and to maximise their effectiveness within lessons.
6. Work effectively as a member of the Department team to improve the quality of teaching and learning.

7. Set high expectations for all pupils, to deepen their knowledge and understanding and to maximise their achievement.

8. Use positive management of behaviour in an environment of mutual respect which allows pupils to feel safe and secure and promotes their self-esteem.

9. To ensure where possible, that appropriate work is set to cover absences.

Monitoring, Assessment, Recording, Reporting and Accountability

1. Be immediately responsible for the processes of identification, assessment, recording and reporting for the pupils in their charge.

2. Contribute towards the planning and recording of appropriate actions and outcomes related to set targets.

3. Assess pupils' work systematically and use the results to inform future planning, teaching and curricular development.

4. Be familiar with statutory assessment and reporting procedures and prepare and present informative, helpful and accurate reports to parents.

5. Keep an accurate register of pupils for each lesson.

Subject Knowledge and Understanding

1. Have a thorough and up-to-date knowledge and understanding of the National Curriculum programmes of study, level descriptors and specifications for examination courses.

2. Keep up-to-date with research and developments in pedagogy and the subject area.

Professional Standards and Development

1. Be a role model to pupils through personal presentation and professional conduct.

2. Arrive in class, on or before the start of the lesson, and begin and end lessons on time.

3. Cover for absent colleagues as is reasonable, fair and equitable.

4. Be familiar with the School and Department handbooks and support all the School's policies, e.g. those on Health and Safety, Citizenship, Literacy, Numeracy and ICT.

5. Establish effective working relationships with all staff.

6. Be involved in extra-curricular activities such as making a contribution to after-school clubs and visits.

7. Maintain a working knowledge and understanding of teachers' professional duties as set out in the current School Teachers' Pay and Conditions document, and teachers' legal liabilities and responsibilities relating to all current legislation, including the role of the education service in safeguarding children.

8. Liaise effectively with parent/carers and with other agencies with responsibility for pupils' education and welfare.

9. Be aware of the role of the Governing Body of the School and support it in performing its duties.

10. Be familiar with and implement the relevant requirements of the current SEN Code of Practice, DDA and Equality Policy.

11. Consider the needs of all pupils within lessons (and implement specialist advice) especially those who:

    - have SEN;
    - are gifted and talented;
    - are not yet fluent in English.

12. Uphold and maintain the practice, ethos and policies of Sunbury Manor School at all times.

Health and Safety

1. Be aware of the responsibility for personal Health, Safety and Welfare and that of others who may be affected by your actions or inactions.
2. Co-operate with the employer on all issues to do with Health, Safety and Welfare.

Continuing Professional Development

1. In conjunction with the line manager, take responsibility for personal professional development, keeping up-to-date with research and developments in teaching pedagogy and changes in the School Curriculum, which may lead to improvements in teaching and learning.
2. Undertake any necessary professional development as identified in the School Improvement Plan taking full advantage of any relevant training and development available.
3. Maintain a professional portfolio of evidence to support the Performance Management process – evaluating and improving own practice.
4. Contribute to the professional development of colleagues.
5. The duties above are neither exclusive nor exhaustive and the post holder may be required by the Head teacher to carry out appropriate duties within the context of the job, skills and grade.

N.B: Every subject teacher will be expected to have pastoral responsibilities.

This job description will be reviewed from time to time and may be subject to amendment or modification at any time after consultation with the post holder. It is not a comprehensive statement of procedures and tasks but sets out the main expectations of the School in relation to the post holder's professional responsibilities and duties.

Sunbury Manor School – Full person specification

	Essential	Desirable
Qualifications and training	• Honours degree • Qualified teacher status	• Good honours degree in the subject that you are teaching
Experience	• Evidence of successful classroom teaching • Proven track record of teaching and motivating all ages and abilities • Ability to demonstrate high standards of classroom practice	• Involvement in working with students in extracurricular activities
Knowledge and understanding	• Awareness of child protection agenda • Able to devise and implement strategies for raising students' achievement in lessons • Committed to continued professional development • Knowledge of National Curriculum • Production of resources to aid effective learning	• Child protection training • Able to develop relevant use of ICT in lessons • Understanding of current issues in learning

(Continued)

195

	Essential	Desirable
Skills	• Ability to motivate and encourage students across the age and ability range • Ability to work successfully as part of a team sharing good practice • Ability to support and help manage change	• Experience of some aspects of whole school initiatives • ICT skills
Teaching and learning	• Knowledge and experience of using a wide range of teaching and learning strategies (including successful use of differentiated material) • Proper use of assessment data to inform teaching and learning • Able to set realistic targets for students' future attainment	• Involvement as a tutor and/ or the delivery of personal, social and health education • Willingness to be involved in the mentoring and evaluating the performance of other staff
Personal attributes	• Demonstrates enthusiasm and sensitivity whilst working with others • Always meets deadlines • Innovative and able to stimulate initiative in others	• Ambitious with a clear Professional Development Plan • Seizes opportunities

(Continued)

Essential	Desirable
• Ambitious for themselves and those with whom they work	• Optimistic and positive
• Communicates an obvious love for their subject and has a strong desire to generate the same attitude in his/her students	
• High personal standards	
• Excellent attendance and punctuality	
• Sense of humour	
• Shows leadership qualities	
• Enthusiastic and lively reflective practitioner	
• Provide positive and appropriate role model for students	
• Forms and maintains appropriate relationships and personal boundaries with students	

BRADLEY STOKE COMMUNITY SCHOOL JOB APPLICATION PACK

The complete job application pack for the role of computing and IT teacher at Bradley Stoke Community School is detailed below.

Bradley Stoke Community School – Full job description

BRADLEY STOKE COMMUNITY SCHOOL
part of the Olympus Academy Trust

ROLE: Computing and IT Teacher

GRADE: Teachers Main or Upper Pay Scale

REPORTS TO: Subject or Curriculum Team Leader

Role profile	Teacher
Job purpose	• To empower students to become independent learners and develop personal responsibilities as a member of the community as described in the BSCS ideal learner profile
	• To facilitate and encourage learning which enables students to achieve high standards
	• To be responsible for the welfare and guidance of students which may include responsibility for a tutor group
Accountabilities (Actions)	**Strategic direction**
	• To take an active role in maintaining the vision and ethos of the school

(Continued)

Role profile	Teacher
	• To implement whole school policies and practices
	• Under the direction of the Curriculum and/or Subject Team Leader, contribute towards short, medium and long-term curriculum plans
	• Ensure that the 4Rs (Reflective, Resilient, Resourceful and Responsible) are explicit in learning and teaching
	Teaching and learning
	• To undertake a designated programme of teaching, ensuring that high quality teaching and learning takes place for all students
	• Support the school self-evaluation
	• Ensure schemes of work are developed and implemented appropriately
	• To carry out necessary assessments and reporting in line with school policy
	• Use systems for the recording, monitoring and target setting of individual students' progress according to department strategies
	• Plan and implement activities to maximise student progress according to their individual needs.
	• To contribute to the enrichment and Session 16 programme

(Continued)

Role profile	Teacher
	• Maintain discipline in accordance with school's behaviour policy and demonstrate good practices in the classes taught with regard to attendance, appearance, uniform, punctuality, behaviour and independent learning (homework)
	• Ensure that independent learning is set, marked and monitored according to the school's policy
	• Ensure that ICT, Literacy and Numeracy are reflected in the teaching and learning experience of students
	• Use a variety of delivery methods that will stimulate learning appropriate to student needs and demands of the learning scheme
	• To mark, grade and give written/verbal and diagnostic feedback as required
	• To ensure the effective deployment of classroom support
	• Contribute to the personal development aspects of the welfare and guidance system including mentoring and tutoring
	• Manage effective rewards and sanctions for students in line with school policy
	Staff development
	• Maintain effective communication across subject teams and with other staff (e.g. Technicians, Student Support team, Learning Support team, Business team etc.)

 (Continued)

Role profile	Teacher

- Engage in the school's continuous professional development programme by participating in arrangements for further training and professional development

- Engage actively in the Appraisal process

- To work as a member of a designated team and to create, maintain and enhance effective working relationships within the school

- Developing community links, including local, national and international networks

Resource management

- Under the direction of the Curriculum and/or Subject Team Leader, prepare, allocate and update resources to support effective learning and teaching within the subject area(s)

- To cooperate with other staff to ensure an effective usage of resources throughout the school

- To ensure processes and practices meet the requirements of Health and Safety policy

Pastoral support

As a tutor:

- To promote a learning focused approach to all tutor activities

(Continued)

Role profile	Teacher
	• To develop learning focused relationships with all members of the tutor group
	• To register students, accompany them to assemblies, encourage their attendance at lessons and their participation in other aspects of school life
	• To monitor the progress of students
	As a teacher:
	• To alert the appropriate staff to problems experienced by the students and to make recommendations as to how these may be resolved
	• To communicate effectively with the parents and carers of students as appropriate
	General
	• To play a full part in the life of the school community, to support its vision and ethos and to encourage staff and students to follow this example
	• To undertake any other duty as specified by the School Teachers Pay and Conditions Document not mentioned in the above
	• Every member of staff should take ownership and responsibility for their health and safety at work and that of others and to ensure that they are appropriately trained for the activity that they are being asked to complete within their job role

(Continued)

Role profile	Teacher
	Whilst every effort has been made to explain the main duties and responsibilities of the post, each individual task undertaken may not be identified.
	Employees will be expected to comply with any reasonable request from a manager/member of the leadership team to undertake work of a similar level that is not specified in this job description.
Knowledge and skills	**Teachers should demonstrate knowledge and understanding of:**

- principles and practices of effective teaching and learning

- preparation of schemes of work and lessons

- knowledge and understanding of subject area(s)

- principles and practices of monitoring/ assessment/evaluation

- the application of ICT to learning and teaching in subject areas

- principles of curriculum planning and associated personalisation techniques to maximise student progress

- cross-curricular themes appropriate to teaching and learning

- learning to learn and thinking skills

(Continued)

Role profile	Teacher	
Support provided	**Line management** A Curriculum or Subject Team Leader will have responsibility for induction and coaching to maximise self-confidence and effectiveness in post	**Wider support** Teachers will participate in local authority best practice forums and the school's professional development programme

Bradley Stoke Community School – Full person specification

BRADLEY STOKE COMMUNITY SCHOOL
Person Specification

Post: Computing & IT Teacher

	Essential	**Desirable**
Qualifications	1. Graduate status and appropriate teaching qualifications	2. Accredited professional development
Experience	1. Evidence of successful teaching which has had a demonstrable impact on student progress	1. Experience of working in a secondary school
	2. Experience of a range of strategies, approaches and resources for developing teaching and learning to meet a wide range of student abilities and needs	2. Training/ expertise in behaviour and/or learning support
		3. Experience of teaching and learning programmes beyond subject boundaries
	3. Evidence of continuing professional development	

(Continued)

	Essential	Desirable
Knowledge, skills and abilities	1. Ability to teach Computing & IT to Key Stage 3 and 4 2. Ability to motivate and inspire students 3. Excellent classroom teacher and interested in developing subject pedagogy 4. Excellent organisational skills 5. Excellent oral and written communication skills 6. Ideas about how to develop personalised learning and how to create independent learners 7. Evidence of collaborative approaches to work (team player) but also able to work independently	1. An ability to teach programming **or** multimedia software skills and concepts up to Key Stage 5 2. Ability to teach Business to Key Stage 4 and 5 3. Able and keen to teach more than one subject 4. An understanding of subject self-evaluation

(Continued)

	Essential	Desirable
	8. Sense of humour, flexibility and ability to remain positive at all times	
	9. Commitment to helping develop, lead and deliver enrichment experiences for all students, including educational visits	
	10. Commitment to working with local primary and secondary schools and community organisations	
	11. Commitment to developing links and networks locally, nationally and internationally	
Health and attendance	1. Record of good health	
	2. Record of excellent timekeeping	

(Continued)

	Essential	Desirable

Supporting information	Ability to:
	
	1. Complete application form, including clear information about which subjects you can teach and to which levels. No CVs will be accepted
	
	2. Fully complete the Skills, Abilities, Knowledge and Experience section of the application or produce a letter of application of no more than 2 sides of A4 stating:
	
	  a) reasons for applying for this post
	
	  b) the skills and experiences you have which are directly related to the post and person specification	

(Continued)

	Essential	Desirable
	c) how you will be involved in developing personalised learning and ensuring that the students become independent learners in Bradley Stoke Community School	
	3. Provide details of two referees who are prepared to support your application, one of whom should be your current employer. Open references will not be accepted	
	4. Return the completed application form and letter, preferably by email, by 9 a.m. on xxx to: vacancies@ bradleystokecs. org.uk	

(Continued)

	Essential	Desirable
	or by post to:	
	Head teacher's name,	
	Head teacher,	
	Bradley Stoke Community School,	
	Fiddlers Wood Lane,	
	Bradley Stoke,	
	South Gloucestershire,	
	BS32 9BS	
	5. Attend for interview in w/c xxx	

Bradley Stoke Community School – Additional information for candidates

The Computing & IT department comprises of three full time teachers, one-part time and one non-specialist. It is a popular option subject at Key Stage 4 and Key Stage 5 and a core curriculum is delivered at Key Stage 3 over three hours a fortnight.

We offer two distinct pathways at KS4: Computer Science (AQA GCSE Computer Science) and Multimedia ICT (TLM INGOTS) so that students can learn skills and develop knowledge in areas they are most interested in. This extends into KS5 where students can elect to study either A Level Computer Science (Eduqas) or a vocational IT course (OCR Cambridge Technicals), which focuses on multimedia-related units. Many of our KS5 students have gone on to study Computing-related degree courses at local and high-profile universities.

KS3 students study an accelerated curriculum that prepares them with the skills, knowledge and understanding required to be successful in their KS4 options courses. KS3 ends in Year 8 and students begin to study their GCSE option choices in Year 9. An outline of the current curriculum is shown on the next page.

The school regards students' access to ICT as important across all subjects. We have subject staff across the curriculum who use ICT extensively in their lessons and are keen to incorporate the fundamentals of good practice, technical skills, knowledge and understanding within their everyday lessons. Our approach is a combination of specialist ICT teaching and a permeation model where all staff are stakeholders in the delivery of high quality ICT. Because we are developing a 21st-century curriculum, our expectation has been that ICT will play a major role in underpinning the learning experience for all students whatever their subject choices. We use our Frog learning platform to deliver material across the curriculum, both within and outside school, as well as streamlining some administrative procedures. Within the department, we make good use of a variety of eLearning tools to support students, including: Frog, Google Drive, Socrative and Blendspace.

There are Promethean ActivBoard interactive white boards in all teaching rooms. There are eight ICT rooms, three other classrooms with desktop PCs and/or Macs. We are currently in the process of initiating a 'bring your own device' (BYOD) scheme to increase student access to ICT in the school, with students being encouraged to use their mobile device (defined as having a 7' screen or bigger and without a cellular signal) in lessons.

The school has an extremely reliable network infrastructure, facilitating 24-hour access for all staff and student members from home. We use Capita SIMS as our school information management system. Additionally, all teaching staff are issued with a laptop and these can be used to access our network via the school-wide wireless cloud.

KEY STAGE 3 CURRICULUM

YEAR 7

We cover:

- 7.1 Introduction to school network
- 7.2 Online Safety Qualification (Students complete a portfolio to achieve a L1 certificate via TLM)
- 7.3 Control Technology (Write algorithms using Flowol)
- 7.4 Spreadsheet Modelling (Develop an interactive quiz in MS Excel)
- 7.5 Databases (Data types, validation and queries; Mail-merge to create Top Trumps cards)

YEAR 8

We cover:

- 8.1 Computer Systems (Input & Output Devices, CPU, Memory, Secondary Storage, Networks)
- 8.2 Control Technology (Write algorithms using Flowol – Year 8 did not study this in Y7)
- 8.3 Web Design (HTML and CSS)
- 8.4 Games Project (Design and develop a game in Scratch)
- 8.5 Our Digital World (Impact of our digital footprint)

KEY STAGE 4 CURRICULUM

GCSE COMPUTER SCIENCE (AQA)

There are two examined components and the first assesses computational thinking, problem solving, code tracing and applied computing. The second examines computer networks, cyber security, ethical, legal and environmental impacts of technology and software development. The non-examined assessment requires students to solve a practical programming problem. Students electing for GCSE Computer Science in years 9 and 10 will start the new AQA specification.

Multimedia ICT (The Learning Machine)

Students complete the five coursework units (pass or fail) outlined below, then take the externally assessed exam to achieve their GCSE grade:

- Unit 1 – IT Productivity
- Unit 4 – IT Security for Users
- Unit 12 – Desktop Publishing
- Unit 15 – Digital Imaging
- Unit 17 – Video Production

KEY STAGE 5 CURRICULUM

A Level Computer Science (Eduqas)

Students who elect for Computer Science at A Level study the full, two-year course which comprises three components:

Component 1:
This component investigates programs, data structures, algorithms, logic, programming methodologies and the impact of computer science on society.

Component 2:
This component investigates computer architecture, communication, data representation, organisation and structure of data, programs, algorithms and software applications.

Component 3:
Students discuss, investigate, design, prototype, refine and implement, test and evaluate a computerised solution to a problem chosen by the candidate which must be solved using original code.

Vocational ICT (OCR Cambridge Technicals)/BTEC Level 3 IT

Students who take Vocational IT in September 2016 will be the first cohort to study the new OCR Cambridge Technicals qualification, with this year's cohort being the last to study Edexcel BTEC Level 3 in IT. We work in partnership with other local Post-16 providers, including schools within the Olympus Academy Trust, to deliver these courses and often teach students from other centres. Contact time is nine hours a fortnight, with one hour dedicated to private study.

Cambridge Technicals (Application Developer Pathway)	BTEC IT
• Fundamentals of IT (exam) • Global Information (exam) • Application Design (mandatory unit) • Internet of Everything • Web Design and Prototyping	• Unit 8 – ecommerce • Unit 29 – Installing Software • Unit 30 – Digital Graphics

ADDITIONAL INFORMATION

Enrichment

Additional activities provided this year include:

- Retro gaming
- Computer club
- Stop Animation
- Android app programming

Teaching Staff

- Subject Team Leader
- Assistant Head: OAT[87] ICT Strategic Lead
- Computing & IT Teacher
- Computing & IT Teacher (Part-Time)
- Subject Team Leader: Business
- Lead TA: Computing & IT, Transition and EAL

APPENDIX 4
CLASS PROFILE FOR USE WITH LESSON AT INTERVIEW

This data is to be used with the 'teaching episode' as described in Chapter 2, Figure 2.5. It helps you to be in control of the learning environment and to cater for the needs of all learners. Take note of pupils with SEN needs – where would they be seated on the seating plan? Why? Consider gender: could this have an impact on where pupils sit in the classroom? Why? What about scores from tests? Would this influence where you seat pupils? Perhaps ability groupings?

Student	Age (years/months)	Gender	SEN need	G&T	PP	Reading score	Spelling score	CATS verbal	CATS non-verbal	CATS quantitative
Student 1	12/2	F								
Student 2	12/6	F				98	118	98	75	96
Student 3	12/6	M				105	114	91	86	98
Student 4	12/0	M		Y		138	101	111	112	117
Student 5	12/6	F		Y		130	118	130	119	117
Student 6	11/10	M				93	91	97	96	91
Student 7	12/6	F				117	96	98	116	103
Student 8	12/7	F	Speech, language or communication need			73	77	83	79	78
Student 9	11/9	M				95	130	112	106	116
Student 10	11/8	F				99	99	97	94	101
Student 11	12/5	F		Y		132	108	134	109	112
Student 12	12/2	F		Y		139	98	120	120	112
Student 13	12/2	F				112	121	111	116	107

Student										
Student 14	11/7	F	Specific learning difficulty			89	69	87	110	76
Student 15	12/1	M				95	97	93	101	106
Student 16	11/7	F				96	117	91	86	88
Student 17	11/8	M				96	92	109	96	103
Student 18	11/11	F				89	77	94	102	99
Student 19	11/11	F				102	101	108	100	97
Student 20	12/0	M				103	98	108	104	95
Student 21	11/9	M	Other difficulty/disability		Y	86	93	101	98	105
Student 22	12/2	M				101	94	106	103	87
Student 23	11/7	F		Y		114	96	123	125	123
Student 24	11/11	M	Aspergers'	Y		133	117	135	133	137
Student 25	11/7	M				95	117	96	97	99
Student 26	12/0	M				86	96	86	100	95
Student 27	12/1	M				100	103	93	102	83
Student 28	12/2	F			Y	99	114	91	102	107
Student 29	11/8	F				96	98	97	93	113
Student 30	12/3	M			Y	108	121	120	122	136

Note: CATS = Cognitive Ability Tests; G&T = Gifted and Talented; PP = Pupil Premium.

APPENDIX 5
PROGRESS GRID

This is an example of a progress grid for pupil self-assessment. It was mentioned in Chapter 3, Figure 3.17 and in the tracking of progress section. This is useful for pupils to see what they should be achieving by topic against their target grade (remember Progress and Attainment 8) and can also aid as an aspirational tool for pupils to see what is required at higher grades.

Topic	Grades 3/2/1 – (D/E/F)	Grades 6/5/4 – (B/C)	Grades 9/8/7 – (A*/A)
Logic Gates and Truth Tables	• **With support,** I can create a truth table for AND, OR and NOT gates	• I can create a truth table for AND, OR, NOT and XOR gates	• I can create a truth table for AND, OR, NOT and XOR gates
	• I can simply explain the importance of simplifying circuits in relation to developing new technologies	• I can explain the importance of simplifying circuits in relation to developing new technologies	• I can explain in detail the importance of simplifying circuits in relation to developing new technologies
	• I can create a simple circuit in a simulator	• I can create a circuit in a simulator	• I can create a detailed circuit in a simulator
	• I have attempted 1 exam-style question	• I have attempted to answer 1–2 exam-style questions	• I have completed 1–2 exam-style questions

Source: http://community.computingatschool.org.uk/resources/3369

APPENDIX 6
LESSON PLAN TEMPLATE

Here's a sample lesson plan you can use for your classes.

Date:		Teacher		LSA:		
Period:		Subject: SOW:		Class:		

Profile of learners:						
Boys	Girls	G&T/More Able	SEN	EAL	PD	Other Notes

Aims and Objectives:		
Last lesson:		
Next lesson:		
All pupils will be able to:	Most pupils will be able to:	Some pupils will be able to:
Resources:	Key words:	Cross-curricular links:

Time:	Individual/Pair/ Group/Class	Activity:	SEN differentiation and extension tasks:

Homework:
Due Date:

Note: Explanation of abbreviations used on the lesson plan – LSA: Learning Support Assistant, SOW: Scheme of Work, G&T: Gifted and Talented, SEN: Special Educational Needs, EAL: English as an Additional Language, PD: Physically Disabled.

APPENDIX 7
SUPPORTING MATERIAL FOR CASE STUDIES

The material here was discussed in Case Study 2 in Chapter 5; this gives visual evidence on how the resources can be implemented.

Collaboration card – as described in Case Study 2:

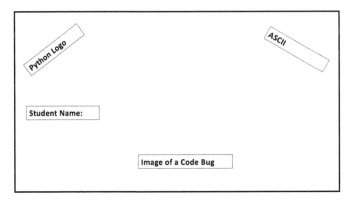

'Collaboration cards' are used to promote an inclusive classroom. With some pre-planning, pupils are easily able to work in groups such as mixed ability, challenged ability and other groups as determined by the teacher. Collaboration cards are also an aid for behaviour management as described in the case study.

Challenge chips display – as described in Case Study 2:

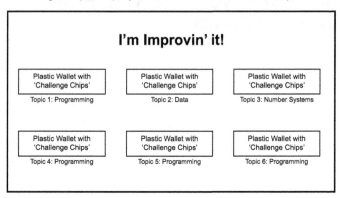

'Challenge chip displays' provide for an element of independent learning, where pupils can choose self-guided pupil challenges from curriculum topics.

Example challenge chip – as described in Case Study 2 (see Morgan, 2015):

An example of what would appear on a challenge chip card, in this case from topic 3, number systems, to foster independent learning.

TOPIC 3 – NUMBER SYSTEMS

Binary arithmetic challenge: The GCSE specification only requires you to do binary addition but it would be good to know how to do binary subtraction as well so that you have a deeper understanding of binary.

Read pages 21 and 22 of the *Binary and Hexadecimal Workbook* and complete the activities on pages 23 to 26.

(Please complete these in your exercise books – do not write in the textbook). Mark your own answers using the QR Codes (you can use your phones for this).

If you need more help, watch the video from Craig 'n' Dave at http://tinyurl.com/cndbinarysub

APPENDIX 8
SUPPORT FOR THE COMPUTER SCIENCE TEACHER (BOOKS, WEBSITES, TOOLS)

As an educator in a subject with fast changing content there is a need to keep abreast of changes in the computing industry as well as changes to your practise. This is even more true in this subject area where you may find yourself being the only specialist in your school or department. Vital to this is networking and reading relevant literature. This section gives some recommendations on starting points.

FOR PRIMARY AND SECONDARY

BBC Bitesize Computational Thinking – short video clips on CT: www.bbc.co.uk/education/topics/z7tp34j/resources/1

BBC Bitesize – material for learners and teachers: www.bbc.co.uk/education

BCS Bookshop – a variety of informative computing titles such as:

- *Computational Thinking* – a book which describes computational thinking and then shows how it is applied directly to programming, using the text-based language Python (Beecher, 2017).[88]

- *BCS Glossary of Computing* – a comprehensive resource covering a wide range of computing terms (BCS Academy Glossary Working Party, 2016).

- *BCS Women in IT* – an ebook featuring current influential women in IT.[89]

Other useful titles include:

- *Cyber Security* (Sutton, 2017)
- *The Internet of Things* (various, 2017)[90]
- *Alan Turing and his Contemporaries* (Lavington, 2012)

Available at http://shop.bcs.org (print books) and Amazon (print and ebooks).

BCS Student Chapters – groups of university students who undertake outreach work in their local communities, such as supporting themed days within school: www.bcs.org/category/18176

BETT – a world-leading education technology show, held annually each January in London, showcasing new advances in education and computing: www.bettshow.com/

CAS – the subject association for computing and computer science teachers. Once on the CAS website you will be able to find information on CAS Regional Centres (CRCs), local CAS Hubs and CAS Regional Conferences: www.computingatschool.org.uk/

CAS Hubs – information on what a CAS Hub offers: http://community.computingatschool.org.uk/hubs

CAS Master Teachers – information on becoming a CAS Master Teacher, what is expected of a CAS Master Teacher and an application form: www.computingatschool.org.uk/custom_pages/36

Citizenship Foundation – for up-to-date information on SMSC, British values and citizenship information: www.doingsmsc.org.uk/

Computer Science for Fun (CS4FN) – a magazine with lots of exciting and creative ways to include computing and computational thinking into lessons such as by magic: www.cs4fn.org/

Digital Schoolhouse – workshops for learners and teachers, using plugged and unplugged activities to teach computer science: www.digitalschoolhouse.org.uk/

Diversity – #include – a subsidiary of CAS, which focuses on computing for all and making the curriculum inclusive: http://casinclude.org.uk/

Education Endowment Foundation – a charity that looks at ways of closing attainment gaps for young people of all backgrounds: https://educationendowmentfoundation.org.uk/resources/teaching-learning-toolkit

Get into teaching – information on how to pursue a career in teaching: https://getintoteaching.education.gov.uk/

Governors – Governors' handbook for governors in maintained schools, academies and free schools: https://www.gov.uk/government/uploads/system/uploads/attachment_data/file/270398/Governors-Handbook-January-2014.pdf

MOOCs – a collation of known MOOCs to support teacher subject knowledge: http://community.computingatschool.org.uk/resources/1489

National curriculum in England: Computing programmes of study – government website which details the statutory programmes of study and attainment for pupils in computing at key stages 1–4: https://www.gov.uk/government/publications/national-curriculum-in-england-computing-programmes-of-study

Physical computing

- **BBC Micro:bit** – resources to support usage of the Micro:bit in the classroom: http://microbit.org/

- **Crumble** – a variety of websites to support usage of the Crumble electronics controller: http://redfernelectronics.co.uk/ and http://community.computingatschool.org.uk/resources/4862

- **MaKey MaKey** – https://learn.sparkfun.com/tutorials/makey-makey-quickstart-guide
- **Picademy** – teacher training available from the Raspberry Pi Foundation: https://www.raspberrypi.org/picademy/

Prevent Duty – departmental advice for schools and childcare providers: https://www.gov.uk/government/uploads/system/uploads/attachment_data/file/439598/prevent-duty-departmental-advice-v6.pdf

Project Quantum – formative assessment questions, for teachers to check pupil understanding and progress: http://community.computingatschool.org.uk/resources/4382

School teachers' pay and conditions 2016 – guidance on school teachers' pay and conditions: https://www.gov.uk/government/uploads/system/uploads/attachment_data/file/550286/STPCD_2016_guidance.pdf

Subject knowledge training guide – 'Subject knowledge requirements for entry into computer science teacher training' – a White Paper which gives guidance on the subject knowledge required across the key stages for successful delivery of the curriculum: www.computingatschool.org.uk/data/uploads/CSSubjectKnowledgeRequirements.pdf

Sutton Trust – an organisation that looks at ways of improving social mobility through education: www.suttontrust.com/

Teachers' perspectives on successful strategies for teaching computing in school – Sue Sentance (sue.sentance@kcl.ac.uk) King's College London, London, UK and Andrew Csizmadia (a.p.csizmadia@newman.ac.uk) Newman University, Birmingham, UK – a paper which looks at pedagogical strategies for teaching the computing curriculum: community.computingatschool.org.uk/files/6769/original.pdf

Teaching London Computing – support for teachers throughout the country through workshops and free classroom resources: https://teachinglondoncomputing.org/

Unions and lesson observation guidance – A Classroom Observation Protocol: Guidelines for NUT School Representatives: www.teachers.org.uk/files/active/0/Observation4798.pdf

Unplugged resources – websites which offer a variety of unplugged activities, covering primary (key stage 1 and key stage 2) and also useful for embedding concepts at secondary level (key stage 3 and key stage 4): http://csunplugged.org/ and https://code.org/curriculum/unplugged

FOR SECONDARY SPECIFICALLY

Awarding bodies:

- AQA – awarding body website with a variety of qualifications, resources and a wealth of information: www.aqa.org.uk/

- OCR – awarding body with a wide range of qualifications, resources and guidance: www.ocr.org.uk/

- WJEC/Eduqas – website offering a wide range of qualifications and resources: www.wjec.co.uk/ or www.eduqas.co.uk/

- Pearson – website encompassing information for Edexcel, BTEC and Pearson LCCI qualifications: https://qualifications.pearson.com/en/home.html

Axsied – computer science books aimed at GCSE, for specific awarding bodies: https://www.axsied.com/

Cambridge GCSE Computing – written material and videos, to support the OCR specification: https://www.cambridgegcsecomputing.org/

Computing in the national curriculum – a guide for secondary teachers: www.computingatschool.org.uk/data/uploads/cas_secondary.pdf

Ebacc – information on computer science in the English Baccalaureate: https://www.gov.uk/government/publications/english-baccalaureate-ebacc/english-baccalaureate-ebacc

Progress 8 – School comparisons – a website on which you can check Progress 8 and Attainment 8 scores: https://www.compare-school-performance.service.gov.uk/compare-schools?phase=secondary

Quick Start Computing – Stage 3 subject knowledge covering the transition from primary to secondary – a guide book to the subject knowledge required at key stage 3, with lots of additional references: http://community.computingatschool.org.uk/files/8213/original.pdf

Teach-ict.com – a website with reading material, videos and games for pupils and teachers to support the new curriculum

Tenderfoot (unplugged resources) – supported by Google for Education, CAS Tenderfoot provides a series of unplugged activities to support and deepen teacher subject knowledge giving rise to use across key stages 3–5: www.computingatschool.org.uk/custom_pages/56-tenderfoot

Websites to help with programming – a list of websites used by practising teachers to support teaching programming:

- https://repl.it/languages/python3
- www.flowgorithm.org/
- https://www.codecademy.com/
- https://www.khanacademy.org/
- https://inventwithpython.com/
- www.101computing.net/
- Craig 'n' Dave: http://craigndave.org/
- http://pynewbs.com/

FOR PRIMARY SPECIFICALLY

Barefoot Computing – supported by CAS, BCS, BT, DfE and the Raspberry Pi Foundation. Barefoot Computing provide support for teachers at primary level through cross-curricular unplugged activities and resources: http://barefootcas.org.uk/

Computing in the national curriculum – a guide for primary teachers: www.computingatschool.org.uk/data/uploads/CASPrimaryComputing.pdf

Primary (key stage 2) performance – a website for teachers to check a school's scores in reading, writing and maths: https://www.compare-school-performance.service.gov.uk/

Quick Start Computing – *A CPD Toolkit for Primary Teachers* – a guidebook to the subject knowledge, planning, teaching and assessment required at primary level: http://primary.quickstartcomputing.org/resources/pdf/qs_handbook.pdf

Websites to help with programming – a list of websites used by practising teachers to support teaching programming:

- https://scratch.mit.edu/
- www.scratchmaths.org/
- https://www.tynker.com/
- http://snap.berkeley.edu/

These resources are not exhaustive, should you find other resources please do share them via the CAS website and through your local CAS Hub. Remember the purpose and mission statement from CAS:

CAS purpose and mission

'Through the participation of the wider community we seek to support and empower each other in an inclusive and self-sustaining body so that each child has the opportunity of an outstanding computer science education. CAS achieves this by supporting and promoting all those individuals, partner organisations, companies, and university departments who wish to run CAS regional hubs, put on CPD courses, generate teaching resources etc. that support the Computing curriculum. There is no "them" – only us.'

Source: www.computingatschool.org.uk/about

NOTES

1. Definition taken from 'Computing in the national curriculum – A guide for secondary teachers': www.computingatschool.org.uk/data/uploads/cas_secondary.pdf

2. The terms foundations, applications and implications are used and described by Miles Berry, Principal Lecturer, University of Roehampton, for additional reading on foundations, applications and implications – http://milesberry.net/2015/10/coding-and-digital-skills/

3. See www.computingatschool.org.uk/custom_pages/32-documents

4. For more detail on how computer science is used in the Ebacc, see https://www.gov.uk/government/publications/english-baccalaureate-ebacc/english-baccalaureate-ebacc

5. Pupils – The term 'pupils' will be used throughout this book as this is what school children are referred to in the programme of study and Department for Education (DfE) publications. However, in school, the word student is also commonly used.

6. The Royal Society report 'divides the subject discipline at school-level into three distinct but interrelated sub-domains: (1) computer science (the rigorous academic discipline that covers algorithms, data structures, programming); (2) digital skills (the general ability to use computers confidently, effectively and safely); and (3) information technology (the design and application

of digital systems to meet user needs for particular purposes). The subject title "computing" is intended to embrace all three of these sub-domains'.

7. See https://royalsociety.org/about-us/

8. https://www.youtube.com/watch?v=kHyLMmPMljg&list =PL6gGtLyXoeq-207fWOMIEO_5JQljJFT5e&index=5

9. https://www.gov.uk/government/speeches/michael-gove-speech-at-the-bett-show-2012

10. http://thelearningcurve.pearson.com/2014-report-summary/

11. An organisation through which governments work to share issues and solve common problems such as educational issues.

12. Early 2017.

13. © Crown 2013.

14. See http://ccea.org.uk/sites/default/files/docs/research_statistics/gcse_draft_proposals/LLW_Draft_Proposals_2016.pdf

15. See https://obamawhitehouse.archives.gov/the-press-office/2016/01/30/fact-sheet-president-obama-announces-computer-science-all-initiative-0

16. Controlled schools are managed and funded by the education authority (EA) through school Boards of Governors (BoGs). Primary and secondary school BoGs consist of representatives of transferors – mainly the Protestant churches – along with representatives of parents, teachers and the EA. For further information on schools in Northern Ireland see https://www.nidirect.gov.uk/articles/types-school#toc-1

17. MOOC, an online learning platform that is available 24 hours a day, supports multimedia and is flexible in meeting learner needs. It allows for unlimited participation and for access across the internet.

18. Outside agencies – examples are social workers, medical staff, attendance officers.

19. Pastoral support involves giving help, support, guidance and information, some of which is directed by the school.

20. A planner is a diary which acts as a link between home and school, so that teachers and parents can communicate.

21. An activity that does not require use of a computer.

22. Please see 'Additional references' section for sources of quotations such as this.

23. '**Spiritual** – Explore beliefs and experience; respect faiths, feelings and values; enjoy learning about oneself, others and the surrounding world; use imagination and creativity; reflect. **Moral** – Recognise right and wrong; respect the law; understand consequences; investigate moral and ethical issues; offer reasoned views. **Social** – Use a range of social skills; participate in the local community; appreciate diverse viewpoints; participate, volunteer and cooperate; resolve conflict; engage with the "British values" of democracy, the rule of law, liberty, respect and tolerance. **Cultural** – Appreciate cultural influences; appreciate the role of Britain's parliamentary system; participate in culture opportunities; understand, accept, respect and celebrate diversity.' www.doingsmsc.org.uk/

24. www.computingatschool.org.uk/data/uploads/CSSubjectKnowledgeRequirements.pdf

25. Beebot – a robot used to assist in teaching children computer science concepts.

26. Feeder school(s) are schools within the catchment/local area. For example, a primary feeder school works with the local secondary school (state or private) to help with pupils transitioning from key stage 2 to 3. The same applies for pupils going from preschool to primary school.

27. https://www.gov.uk/government/uploads/system/uploads/attachment_data/file/301107/Teachers__Standards.pdf

28. Central Processing Unit (CPU) – the 'brain' of the computer where processing takes place.

29. 'The pupil premium is additional funding for publicly funded schools in England to raise the attainment of disadvantaged pupils of all abilities and to close the gaps between them and their peers': https://www.gov.uk/guidance/pupil-premium-information-for-schools-and-alternative-provision-settings

30. Open evenings: schools are opening to the public usually once a year and each department has an exhibition of the best that they can offer across the key stages.

31. Options evenings: usually take place mid-way through year 9, and include an evening where parents and their children visit each department within the school to see what the department offers for key stage 4.

32. http://socialissues.cs.toronto.edu/

33. CS4FN has published a resource on magic tricks that can be used in the classroom. See Appendix 8.

34. A supply teacher is a substitute teacher who teaches at short notice when regular members of staff are absent. Supply teachers in many cases are unfamiliar with the structure or layout of the school.

35. Computer science is the subject examinable at GCSE and not computing.

36. Blooms Taxonomy – created by Dr Benjamin Bloom, an educational psychologist, to promote higher order thinking. The taxonomy shows low level thinking skills such as knowledge and comprehension to higher order thinking skills such as application, analysis, synthesis and evaluation.

37. **OFSTED** is the Office for Standards in Education, Children's Services and Skills.

38. Progress 8 is a relatively new measure; the following website can be used for obtaining progress 8 scores – https://www.compare-school-performance.service.gov.uk/compare-schools?phase=secondary

39. Key stage 2 performance for primary schools can be found at https://www.compare-school-performance. service.gov.uk/

40. www.bcs.org/category/17784

41. https://www.sfia-online.org/en/sfia-6/skills/procurement-management-support/skill-management/teaching-and-subject-formation

42. https://www.sfia-online.org/en/sfia-6/skills/procurement-management-support/skill-management/teaching-and-subject-formation

43. SLT – typically comprises the head teacher, deputy and assistant head teachers.

44. https://www.teachers.org.uk/edufacts/appraisal

45. https://www.gov.uk/government/uploads/system/uploads/attachment_data/file/583857/Progress_8_school_performance_measure_Jan_17.pdf

46. Primary key stage 2 performance in reading, writing and maths: https://www.compare-school-performance. service.gov.uk/

47. AfL techniques are those for formative learning.

48. Scribe video is creating an animation to tell a story (topic) in a fun way. This can be in the form of drawing concepts on the board as you explain them to the class.

49. OCR MOOC: https://www.cambridgegcsecomputing.org/

50. Future Learn: https://www.futurelearn.com/courses/teaching-computing-stem

51. In the early days of your teaching career it is advisable to annotate your lesson plan with timings to ensure that you and the pupils stay on task. There are many different versions of lesson plans and Appendix 6 gives an example of a lesson plan which allows for timings.

52. Digital Schoolhouse use a combination of plugged and unplugged activities to teach computer science.

53. See the CAS TV video at https://www.youtube.com/watch?v=y82kfmS3xCA for further discussion. Also one annual event is that being run by Professor Peter Kemp at Roehampton University who holds a 3D Animation summer school for pupils at key stages 4 and 5. See www.3dami.org.uk/

54. Note that at GCSE level the exam subject is referred to as computer science.

55. The literature web is a model used to guide pupils through interpreting and understanding a piece of text.

56. Prevent duty – there is guidance for different parts of the UK: https://www.gov.uk/government/publications/prevent-duty-guidance

57. Progress grids; see http://community.computingatschool.org.uk/resources/3369

58. As this book is published in black and white, the solid grey represents green, the dots represent amber and the lines represent red.

59. The pupil premium is additional funding for publicly-funded schools in England to raise the attainment of disadvantaged pupils of all abilities and to close the gaps between them and their peers. This covers free school meals (FSM), FSM 6-pupils who have had FSM in the past six years, looked after children (LAC) and adopted children.

60. VLE – an online learning platform that allows you to put a variety of media (text, images, podcasts, animations, videos) online to support both in and out of class learning.

61. Free to BCS members and only £2.99 to purchase for non-members.

62. A MOOC is an online learning platform that is available 24 hours a day, supports multimedia and is flexible to meet learner needs; it allows for unlimited participation and for access across the internet.

63. Accessibility settings – features to help manage a disability.

64. The Individual Education Plan is a document that is developed for pupils that have special education needs. The plan is reviewed at set intervals to ensure that it is up-to-date and effective.

65. British Values are democracy, the rule of law, individual liberty, and mutual respect and tolerance of those with different faiths and beliefs; see 'Additional references'.

66. https://educationendowmentfoundation.org.uk/

67. The Sutton Trust – this is a charity that looks at improving social mobility through education.

68. https://www.researchgate.net/publication/311595274_The_Roehampton_Annual_Computing_Education_Report_2015_data_from_England

69. https://www.gov.uk/government/publications/school-teachers-pay-and-conditions-2016

70. INSET – In Service Training day; pupils are not in school. Teachers are in school and receive training.

71. Sets – these are groupings by ability, which allow for differentiation between sets. Some schools, however, have mixed ability groups all the way through key stage 3, which then require further differentiation within the set.

72. The cover example given here is for secondary school; covers can also occur in primary school.

73. In primary school, teachers have a class for which they are responsible. The term tutor group is used at secondary level.

74. Afterschool detentions occur at secondary school along with isolation. In primary school other methods are employed, such as isolation during the day.

75. Options evenings usually take place mid-way through year 9, when pupils attend with their parents and visit each subject area and teacher to find out what taking that subject at GCSE level entails.

76. Many primary schools tend to buy in IT Support and do not have an onsite person.

77. Seven segment display – an electronic display based upon binary numbers that displays decimal numbers 0–9, used in displays such as those on digital clocks and calculators.

78. Crumble – a small electronic programmable board.

79. More information on SKEs is available at: https://getintoteaching.education.gov.uk/explore-my-options/teacher-training-routes/subject-knowledge-enhancement-ske-courses

80. School experience: https://getintoteaching.education.gov.uk/school-experience

81. Scheme of Work – shows what is to be achieved in a subject or year group in an academic year; typically included are week numbers, topics, objectives, teacher activity, student activity, learning outcomes, cross-curricular links, differentiation, resources, and so on.

82. A store selling computer equipment.

83. Elon Reeve Musk is a South African-born Canadian-American business magnate, investor, engineer and inventor: https://en.wikipedia.org/wiki/Elon_Musk

84. Source: www.independent.co.uk/life-style/gadgets-and-tech/news/elon-musk-ai-artificial-intelligence-computer-simulation-gaming-virtual-reality-a7060941.html

85. IT Support is used here for managing the network.

86. FakeBot – a paper-based cut-out of a Beebot.

87. OAT = Olympus Academy Trust.

88. For GCSE, A-level.

89. www.bcs.org/upload/pdf/women-it.pdf

90. Ebook only.

REFERENCES

BCS Academy Glossary Working Party (2016) *BCS Glossary of Computing* (14th edition). BCS Learning and Development Ltd, Swindon.

Beecher, K. (2017) *Computational Thinking – A Beginner's Guide to Problem Solving and Programming*. BCS Learning and Development Ltd, Swindon.

Brookshear, G. and Brylow, D. (2014) *Computer Science: An Overview: Global Edition*. Pearson, Harlow.

Morgan, D. (2015) *Binary and Hexadecimal Workbook for GCSE Computer Science and Computing: Volume 1* (Comp Sci Workbooks). Lessonhacks.com.

ADDITIONAL REFERENCES

3D animation

- University of Roehampton (2015) News – Lecturer awarded funding to expand 3D animation summer school. Available from: https://www.roehampton. ac.uk/education/news/lecturer-awarded-funding-to-expand-3d-animation-summer-school/ (accessed February 2017).

British values

- Gov.uk (2014) Promoting fundamental British values as part of SMSC in schools' Departmental advice for maintained schools. Available from: https:// www.gov.uk/government/uploads/system/uploads/ attachment_data/file/380595/SMSC_Guidance_ Maintained_Schools.pdf (accessed March 2017).

Careers

- Primary Futures/NAHT A guide for primary school leaders on working with employers and volunteers (2014) Available from: www.educationandemploers. org/wp-content/uploads/2014/10/Primary-Guide-FINAL.pdf (accessed January 2017).

Case studies

- Independent Newspaper (2016) Elon Musk: The chance we are not living in a computer simulation is 'one in

billions'. Available from: www.independent.co.uk/
life-style/gadgets-and-tech/news/elon-musk-ai-
artificial-intelligence-computer-simulation-gaming-
virtual-reality-a7060941.html (accessed February
2017).

- Gr8Computing Blog (2017) Chris Sharples. Available
from: www.gr8computing.com/ (accessed February
2017).

- TED – Ideas worth spreading (2016) Reshma Saujani:
Teach girls bravery, not perfection. Available from:
https://www.ted.com/talks/reshma_saujani_teach_
girls_bravery_not_perfection (accessed February
2017).

Computational thinking definition

- Wing, J. (2014) Computational thinking benefits
society. Social Issues in Computing. Available from:
http://socialissues.cs.toronto.edu/ (accessed May
2017).

CPD

- Gov.uk (2014) National Professional Qualification
for Senior Leadership (NPQSL). Available from:
https://www.gov.uk/guidance/national-professional-
qualification-for-senior-leadership-npqsl (accessed
October 2015).

- Gov.uk (2014) National Professional Qualification
for Middle Leadership (NPQML). Available from:
https://www.gov.uk/guidance/national-professional-
qualification-for-middle-leadership-npqml (accessed
October 2015).

- Gov.uk (2017) Head teacher (NPQH). Available from:
https://nationalcareersservice.direct.gov.uk/job-
profiles/headteacher (accessed March 2017).

Curriculum changes

- Department for Education and The Rt. Hon **Michael Gove MP** (2012). Available from: https://www.gov.uk/government/speeches/michael-gove-speech-at-the-bett-show-2012 (accessed November 2016).

- National Curriculum in England: Computing programmes of study (2013). Available from: https://www.gov.uk/government/publications/national-curriculum-in-england-computing-programmes-of-study/national-curriculum-in-england-computing-programmes-of-study#key-stage-3 (accessed November 2016).

- Pearson (2014) The learning curve – Top education systems. Available from: http://thelearningcurve.pearson.com/2014-report-summary/ (accessed November 2016).

- Welsh Government (2013) The ICT Steering Group's report to the Welsh Government. Available from: http://learning.gov.wales/resources/browse-all/ict-steering-groups-report/?lang=en (accessed November 2016).

- Professor Graham Donaldson CB (2015) Successful futures: Independent review of curriculum and assessment arrangements in Wales. Available from: http://gov.wales/docs/dcells/publications/150317-successful-futures-en.pdf (accessed November 2016).

- Governors Wales (2016) A curriculum for Wales – A curriculum for life. Available from: www.governorswales.org.uk/ (accessed November 2016).

- Royal Society (2012) Shut down or restart – The way forward for computing in UK schools. Available from: https://royalsociety.org/~/media/education/computing-in-schools/2012-01-12-computing-in-schools.pdf (accessed November 2016).

- Royal Society (2012) Shut down or restart. Available from: https://royalsociety.org/topics-policy/projects/computing-in-schools/report/ (accessed November 2016).

- Gov.uk (2013) Consultation report. Available from: https://www.gov.uk/government/uploads/system/uploads/attachment_data/file/193838/CONSULTATION_REPORT_CHANGING_ICT_TO_COMPUTING_IN_THE_NATIONAL_CURRICULUM.pdf (accessed November 2016).

- About PLAN C (2013) Professional learning and networking for computing – Scotland. Available from: http://academy.bcs.org/content/computing-scottish-schools and www.cas.scot/plan-c/ (accessed November 2016).

- Naace, ITTE, and the Computing at School Working Group (2012) ICT and Computer Science in UK Schools. Available from: www.computingatschool.org.uk/custom_pages/32-documents (accessed November 2016).

Curriculum differences

- Michael Jones FRSA, Winston Churchill Fellow (2015) Developing a computer science curriculum in England: Exploring approaches in the USA. Available from: www.wcmt.org.uk/sites/default/files/report-documents/Jones%20M%20Report%202015%20%20Final.pdf (accessed January 2017).

- Computer Science Teachers Organisation (2016) Available from: https://www.csteachers.org/ (accessed January 2017).

- College Board (2016) AP computer science principles. Available from: https://secure-media.collegeboard.org/digitalServices/pdf/ap/ap-computer-science-principles-course-and-exam-description.pdf (accessed February 2017).

- Citizens Advice Scotland (2015) Types of school. Available from: https://www.citizensadvice.org.uk/scotland/family/education/school-and-pre-school-education-s/types-of-school-s/ (accessed March 2017).

- Education Scotland (2016). Available from: https://education.gov.scot/scottish-education-system (accessed March 2017).

- Qualifications Wales (2016). Available from: http://qualificationswales.org/?lang=en (accessed March 2017).

Diversity

- Google Inc and Gallup Inc (2016) Diversity gaps in computer science: Exploring the underrepresentation of girls, Blacks and Hispanics. Available from: http://services.google.com/fh/files/misc/diversity-gaps-in-computer-science-report.pdf (accessed February 2017).

- #include Computer Science for All (2016). Available from: http://casinclude.org.uk/ (accessed January 2017).

- Kemp, Peter, Wong, Billy and Berry, Miles (2016) The Roehampton annual computing education report. Available at: https://www.researchgate.net/publication/311595274_The_Roehampton_Annual_Computing_Education_Report_2015_data_from_England (accessed February 2017).

- BBC (2017) www.bbc.co.uk/sport/football/premier-league/table (accessed February 2017).

Governors

- NGA (2017) Representing and supporting governors from state funded schools. Available from: www.nga.org.uk/Home.aspx (accessed February 2017).

Jobs

- BCS (2016) Applying for teaching jobs – BCS Academy of Computing. Available from:

  http://academy.bcs.org/teachingjobs (accessed January 2017).

- Try Teaching (2016) Graduate teacher internship scheme. Available from: www.tryteaching.org/ (accessed March 2017).

Lesson observation

- National Union of Teachers (2017) Appraisal and classroom observation. Available from: https://www.teachers.org.uk/edufacts/appraisal (accessed May 2017).

Literature web

- The Centre for Gifted Education, School of Education. The College of William and Mary (2008) Teaching and learning model – The literature web. Available from: www.scusd.edu/sites/main/files/file-attachments/lit_web.pdf (accessed February 2017).

Maker spaces

- Provenzano, Nicholas (2016) *Your Starter Guide to Maker Spaces (The Nerdy Teacher Presents)*. Blend.

Maths

- BBC Bitesize (2014) Geometry and measures. Available from: www.bbc.co.uk/schools/gcsebitesize/maths/geometry/polygonsrev5.shtml (accessed January 2017).

Pedagogy

- Cockburn, Alistair and Williams, Laurie (2000) The costs and benefits of pair programming. Available from: https://collaboration.csc.ncsu.edu/laurie/Papers/XPSardinia.PDF (accessed January 2017).

- Queen Mary University of London (2011) Available from: www.cs4fn.org/faces/emotionmachine.pdf (accessed February 2017).

Pupil premium

- Gov.uk (2016) Pupil premium: Funding and accountability for schools. Available from: https://www.gov.uk/guidance/pupil-premium-information-for-schools-and-alternative-provision-settings (accessed January 2017).

Quotes

- Beverly Clarke – Author and Subject Matter Expert

  - 'Responding to change is a basic teacher skill.'

  - 'Organisation is affective and effective.'

  - 'Celebrate the positive in every day. It is always there, even when we have to look harder on some days.'

- Steve Clarke – Director of Computing and Curriculum Consultant

  - 'Have a practical element to every lesson. Unplugged resources are key!'

  - 'Think of your lesson in the language of the pupils. "Is your lesson RINGing or MINGing?" (RINGing – Relevant, Interesting, Naughty or a Giggle).'

  - 'Upon taking up my post, I was the department. It took a few months to settle into post and to let my personality shine through into my teaching.'

- Kathie Drake – Year 2 Teacher/Computing Subject Co-ordinator

  - 'We are teaching children for jobs that don't exist. So, everything has to be about building resilience, problem solving and collaboration.'

  - 'When I was 16 I learnt to touch type. I knew I wasn't going to be a secretary, but it was a skill for the future. This is exactly the same concept being applied to computer science and computational thinking.'

- Jayne Fenton-Hall – Head of IT and Computing, CAS Master Teacher and Hub Leader

  - 'I wish I had realised how many pupils come from a difficult or challenging background. I was unprepared for the number of pupils for whom education is not the priority.'

  - 'All schools are not the same. The routines, timings and structure can be hugely different.'

- Steven Gibson – Year 5 Teacher, Primary Computing Co-ordinator, CAS Master Teacher and Hub Leader

  - 'Teaching is all about verbalising passion to make the lesson contagious.'

- Chris Sharples – Head of Computing, CAS Master Teacher and Hub Leader

  - 'My most satisfied moments in teaching are what I call GOTCHA Moments when a student makes a connection or "gets" an idea.'

  - 'Overall, I believe that techniques that are good for subsets of students are good for ALL students.'

Resources

- Various (2017) CAS TV – Available from: https://www.youtube.com/user/computingatschool (accessed January 2017).

- A-level binary addition and subtraction. Available from: https://www.youtube.com/watch?v=ic5ec92cB QE&list=PLCiOXwirraUBO3Z2dxnIfuNDspmJmorJB&i ndex=5 (accessed February 2017) or available from: http://tinyurl.com/cndbinarysub

- Morgan, D. (2015) *Binary and Hexadecimal Workbook for GCSE Computer Science and Computing: Volume 1* (Comp Sci Workbooks). Lessonhacks.com.

School governors

- The Key for School Governors (2017) Information, guidance and resources for school governors. Available from: https://schoolgovernors.thekeysupport.com/ (accessed February 2017).

- National Governors Association (2017) Available from: www.nga.org.uk/Home.aspx (accessed February 2017).

Schools in Northern Ireland

- NI Direct Government Services (2017) Types of school. Available from: https://www.nidirect.gov.uk/articles/ types-school#toc-1 (accessed May 2017).

Standards

- SFIA Foundation (2015) The Skills Framework for the Information Age – SFIA. Available from: https:// www.sfia-online.org/en and https://www.sfia-online. org/en/how-sfia-works/responsibilities-and-skills (accessed February 2017).

- BCS (2017) SFIAplus – Competitive advantage through structured skill development. Available from: www. bcs.org/upload/pdf/sfiaplus-flyer.pdf (accessed February 2017).

- SFIA Foundation (2015) The Skills Framework for the Information Age – SFIA. Available from: https://www.sfia-online.org/en/sfia-6/skills/procurement-management-support/skill-management/teaching-and-subject-formation (accessed May 2017).

- OFSTED – Office for Standards in Education. Available from: https://www.gov.uk/government/organisations/ofsted/about (accessed March 2017).

- Progress 8 and Attainment 8 – School performance measures. Available from: https://www.gov.uk/government/uploads/system/uploads/attachment_data/file/583857/Progress_8_school_performance_measure_Jan_17.pdf (accessed March 2017).

Teachers' standards and guidance documents

- Gov.uk (2013) Teachers' standards guidance for school leaders, school staff and governing bodies. Available from: https://www.gov.uk/government/uploads/system/uploads/attachment_data/file/301107/Teachers__Standards.pdf (accessed February 2017).

- Gov.uk (2013) Teacher's standards. Available from: https://www.gov.uk/government/publications/teachers-standards (accessed May 2017).

- Gov.uk (2016) School teachers' pay and conditions document 2016 and guidance on school teachers' pay and conditions. Available from: https://www.gov.uk/government/uploads/system/uploads/attachment_data/file/550286/STPCD_2016_guidance.pdf (accessed February 2017).

- Gov.uk (2016) Get into teaching. Available from: https://getintoteaching.education.gov.uk/funding-and-salary/teacher-salaries (accessed February 2017).

- National Union of Teachers (2005) Planning, preparation and assessment (PPA) time, leadership and management time: Guidance for NUT members. Available from: https://www.teachers.org.uk/files/PPA_207sq%20(3996).pdf (accessed February 2017).

- UCAS (2017) UCAS teacher training entry requirements. Available from: https://www.ucas.com/ucas/teacher-training/getting-started/ucas-teacher-training-entry-requirements (accessed May 2017).

- UCL Engineering (2013) Teenagers create computer-animated film shorts at UCL Engineering. Available from: www.engineering.ucl.ac.uk/news/teenagers-create-computer-animated-film-shorts-at-ucl-engineering/ (accessed February 2017).

Technical terminology

- BCS Academy Glossary Working Party (2016) *BCS Glossary of Computing* (14th edition). BCS Learning and Development Limited, Swindon.

Unions

- NASUWT – The Teachers Union (2017) Available from: https://www.nasuwt.org.uk/ (accessed January 2017).

- NUT – National Union of Teachers (n.d.) Available from: https://www.teachers.org.uk/ (accessed January and March 2017).

Video Scribe

- Manchester Metropolitan University (2017) Available from: www.mmu.ac.uk/sas/bssg/Modal%20pages/vsmodal.html (accessed February 2017).

INDEX